All in the Family

All in the Family

Parenting the 1950s Way

ELIZABETH LONGFORD

FOREWORD BY RACHEL BILLINGTON

First published 1954
This edition published 2008

The History Press Ltd
The Mill, Brimscombe Port,
Stroud, Gloucestershire, GL5 2QG
www.thehistorypress.co.uk

British Library Cataloguing in Publication Data.
A catalogue record for this book is available from the British Library.

ISBN 978 0 7509 5066 4

Typesetting and origination by The History Press Ltd
Printed in Great Britain

Contents

Foreword

I was eleven when my mother put together this book. I was number five in a family of eight children, four girls and four boys. We lived in a tall ugly house in Chelsea and in a beautiful Georgian house in Sussex, inherited by my father.

We were a loud, argumentative family; the five youngest, including me, went to Catholic day schools in London. My mother was a woman of great intellect, energy and charm.

If she'd been living now, instead of in the early 1950s, I think it inconceivable she wouldn't have had a long-lasting political career. She set off to be a politician, standing for parliament as a Labour candidate, but eventually, for a mixture of reasons, she gave it up and turned her attention to her children.

I wouldn't, however, describe it as all her attention. She remained involved in politics and various public good works. Some of my least comfortable memories as a self-conscious child are of her speaking at fêtes or schools, her voice made strident by the lack of a microphone. Every year she opened our village fête and every year I spent weeks turning myself into a sweetpea or a butterfly in high hopes, if not certainty, of winning the fancy dress competition. As disappointment piled on disappointment, and my sweetpeas elaborated into hollyhocks and my butterflies into bumble bees, I realised at last that my mother would never give her own child a prize.

She did make a point of always being at home at tea-time when we returned from school. She also drove us in a windowless Dormobile van to Sussex every Friday evening, which was heroic considering my habit of being sick over treasured possessions and our joy in quarrelling more or less non-stop. We did stop: once to spend our weekly sweet money and once to eat our picnic of white baps and processed cheese. We were all, I may say, extremely healthy on this diet. My mother's second-favourite filling was sandwich spread.

Her mothering did not include cooking, cleaning, shopping or washing, which was done by a succession of cooks and au pairs who were loved or tortured by us according to their just desserts—or at least our view of their just desserts. Two of these noble women stayed with us to my parents' last gasp and are still alive: Gwendolyn and Ellen, I salute your skills.

My mother's skills were very obvious to us and we were enormously proud of the things she did instead of making us cottage pies. She probably started writing, like so many women, because she could do it in the home. Eventually she became a biographer, writing classic biographies of Queen Victoria and the Duke of Wellington amongst others. Her concentration was so good that she could produce a newspaper article or, in later years, a page or two of a book, with quantities of restless children filling the room.

I can remember very well when she started writing the pieces for Beaverbrook's *Daily Express* which eventually were turned into this book, originally titled *Points for Parents*. We thought it great fun that we were the material for a real book. We didn't bother to read it, of course, or we would have seen that for every reference to one of our childhood foibles, there were many more taken from her devoted readers' letters.

My personal copy was signed lovingly with the advice to see p. 134. So I did turn to p. 134 and read: 'At two years old, Rachel was a fierce biter but has turned into the most calm and sanguine of the children.' Frankly, I'm not sure which characteristic I prefer.

My mother was an excellent journalist. She brought to her writing her deep sympathy and interest in people—whether they were family or stranger, ninety years old or nine. Even after her death I often meet people who feel they were her best friend because she had helped them in some special, imaginative and loving way.

She brought this approach to her writing about children. Whether she is discussing jealousy, teenage parties, night fears or aggression, she tackles the subject with a mixture of common sense and intelligence. Most important of all, she is determined to see things just as much from the child's point of view as the mother's—an attitude remarkable for the time. Although not against discipline when necessary, she assumes the child to be a good, interesting human being capable of every kind of success. In this, the book reflects her own optimistic approach to life, which she never lost over the ninety-six years of her life.

It would be hard to deny that the book is in one sense a period piece. My mother is discussing whether children should be allowed to read comics, rather than whether they should be allowed to play violent computer games. Even television was so new an institution that she didn't think it worth writing about. The book is aimed at the English middle classes during the middle of the century at a time when houses had pantries and a husband was a remote breadwinner, only called in as a father in the last resort. Famously, my own father once admired a pretty baby in a pram only to be told it was his own child. His pocket money hand-outs included all children in the house to avoid having to pick out his own. Occasionally, my mother's take on things raises a wry smile. For example she suggests that it is fine for children to read comics as long as they turn to Keats as well. Oh for those halcyon days! So there are those who may be drawn to this book as to an historical document, the record of an era long past, charming but no longer applicable.

But that is to miss two basic points about the book: firstly, her understanding of children's needs goes far beyond any particular time or place; and secondly, she is able to turn her views into practical advice. I'll give just one illustration of this which also shows her thoroughness once she got onto a subject she cared about.

My mother believed deeply in the importance of reading, and a love of reading is probably the most important gift she gave all her own children, and possibly the reason so many of us became writers, since reading and writing are inextricably entwined. But her advice is utterly practical and is, as so often in this book, divided into individual points. One section is headed 'The Art of Reading Aloud'—notice the use of the word 'Art'!—and throws up no less than eight pieces of advice, all with at least a paragraph of explanation:

1 Have a regular time every day for reading
2 Always have the children really close to you when reading
3 Small children need pictures on every page (publishers note)
4 Don't try reading long stories aloud till the children are of school age
5 Don't worry if your children demand to be read the same book over and over again
6 Encourage older siblings to read to younger
7 Reading needn't stop altogether even when children are in their teens
8 Adults can read aloud to each other too

There follows a list of classic books for younger children, most of which would still be on a contemporary list and, if not, should be.

Her eight rules do not include the joys of reading in the open air. On one memorable occasion she drove us five younger children to Tintern Abbey expressly so that we should read the great poem from the spot where Wordsworth had sat as he composed it. Rain, stinging nettles, barbed wire, a herd of curious bullocks and no certainty where the poet had positioned himself did not deter her. We read the poem; in fact, I read the poem, as proved by a photograph, and if honesty compels me to admit that we all look both bored and rebellious, we never forgot the experience.

Throughout the book, little snippets of brilliance jump off the pages: for those who are worried about children receiving too many presents at Christmas, make sure they give as well as receive—little cheap things or things they have made themselves; if a little boy wants to hit his sister, tell him to pummel the sofa instead; a ten-year-old who cuts his knee gets far more sympathy than a teenager who feels moody and yet the plight of the second is more to be pitied.

As I was growing up, I grew accustomed to peoples' wondering looks when I told them I was one of eight children. Usually I interpreted this as admiration or even jealousy; sometimes I couldn't avoid seeing the criticism. I can still remember my outrage when my mother received a letter accusing her of breeding like a rabbit. But nobody ever asked why she wanted so many children nor did I ever ask her.

Looking at this book so many years after it was written, I think the answer is there: my mother thought human life at all stages absolutely fascinating, whether babies, children or adults. Nothing gave her greater pride and pleasure than to bring another human being into the world, then guide their development and growth. This book allows the reader to share her enjoyment and learn from her wisdom.

Rachel Billington
September 2008

Introduction to the Original Edition

Dear Fellow Parents,

This book is very unassuming. If I were a qualified doctor, psychiatrist, nurse, teacher or social worker I should not feel so humble. I should feel that my practical experience as a mother had the right kind of backing. As it is, I present my 'points', unbacked, to the ordinary non-specialist world from which they come. The world of parents and children; of home. They are part of a mixed harvest gathered over a period of twenty-one years.

Most of them have been published in the *Daily Express*, to whom my thanks are due for kind permission to use them here, in considerably amplified form.

I am also grateful to the Revd R. Gorman, C.P., Editor of *The Sign*, New Jersey, U.S.A., for allowing me to include part of an article first published in his magazine.

I suppose there are some advantages in this kind of non-professional book. At least you will get advice based on the experiences of a normal family. We have had the usual ration of ill-health and other troubles. But also as much or more success than we deserved. The parents of these children have had the normal number of outside interests—perhaps rather above the average on the mother's side, for I have tried at different periods to combine motherhood with a career. But I think I can honestly say that we, like so many thousands of other parents, have tried to put our children's interests first.

I should add that your letters from which I quote were also written in the atmosphere of ordinary life. I was not appealed to as a scientific expert on children's upbringing, but simply as another mother interested in the myriad problems of a normal home.

You can see from the small size of this collection that only a tiny fraction of the problems that face us can find a place here. There is no chapter, for instance, devoted to religious teaching. I shall hope to write about this all-important subject on a future occasion. Even the subjects I do touch on are certainly not dealt with exhaustively. But I don't think this really matters, for a reason I shall now explain.

Personally, I have always been an avid reader of books, magazines and articles about children. I have found there are two different ways in which this reading can be of enormous help. First, we can get concrete advice on particular problems. We can get answers to the actual questions that bother us. That is very useful, and I hope some parents will find some answers in this book. But I've never found that was the only pleasure or even chief pleasure I got from reading about children.

My chief delight was in the interest, enthusiasm and increased keenness it generated in me, a mother, for my task of bringing up a family. After a 'good read' I would feel a new determination to do better in the future. I would feel encouraged and even excited. All my hopes for this book will be satisfied if it can produce similar enthusiasm for their job in other parents.

I have found the writings and conversation of child psychologists and psychiatrists immensely stimulating and helpful. But in one important matter I believe parents must go beyond them. Mothers and fathers must teach their children to be *good*. To be well-adjusted and well-balanced is not enough. A well-adjusted person could be extremely selfish. Conversely, some of the saints were maladjusted to a degree. Of course I do not therefore mean that parents should adopt a plan of instilling sanctity through misery. We hope that our children will be happy as well as good. But I do suggest that to regard them as little machines, which we must keep well-oiled and assist to work smoothly for whatever mysterious or inexplicable purpose, is not the full idea of parenthood.

There seems to be a fairly widespread tendency among psychologists to deny that children are ever 'naughty' (or for that matter, ever 'good'). Some of them express this view by saying that they do not believe in 'original sin'. Most so-called 'naughtiness' is due, in their eyes, to the parents' mishandling. A few go further and admit that the parents are not to blame either, for *their* parents have in turn mishandled them (I often wonder how far back, on this theory, one has to go to find where the trouble began. Naturally not to our first parents, Adam and Eve, for on this account they were only invented to explain 'original sin'. Perhaps it all started when some unlucky protoplasm divided itself hurriedly, without due care for the personality of the emergent ego.)

My own view is the accepted Christian one. Namely, that we are all born with a slant towards wrong-doing; but also with free-will and a strong hope of supernatural help. A Christian can easily agree with the psychologists that maladjusted parents are likely to produce maladjusted children. But a Christian parent cannot agree that there is no such thing as a bad child. It is precisely his business to help his family to be good.

Again, this is far from implying that any child is ever bad in an absolute or even predominant sense. I would not agree with one correspondent, a father, who wrote, 'Some children have not a redeeming feature in their make-up.' We are all made in the same image, and we must respect our Maker in every human personality. But at certain moments in every child's life, as in every grown-up's too, Christian parents are bound to recognise that the devil is having a bit of a break. Of course our own mishandling may have given him his chance. Nevertheless we must face the fact that sometimes he is there. On these occasions our main concern is how to drive him out. And, as I shall hope to show in the chapters that follow, our greatest weapon is love.

It is a doctor's job to make people healthy, not to make them good. Most psychiatrists have been trained as doctors. Perhaps that is one reason why they sometimes seem to err in reducing genuine problems of morals to technical defects in organising one's personality.

I must end with a personal note. I have decided usually to call my children by their real names in the pages that follow. The alternatives were to give them *noms de plume*—a horrid practice—(I once called my daughter Antonia 'Belinda' in an article. She strongly objected!) or to refer to them as 'my five-year-old', 'my youngest daughter', 'my second son', etc.—a somewhat clumsy device. It is simpler to use real names, as do so many parents who write to me.

Four of mine are girls and four are boys. Here are their names and ages: Antonia 21; Thomas 30; Patrick 16; Judith 13; Rachel 11; Michael 10; Catherine 8; Kevin 6. The older ones would like to take this opportunity of saying that all the opinions expressed in this book are entirely those of their mother. And I would like, in turn, to thank them for allowing me to use them as raw material, and in many cases for recalling incidents I had forgotten or never known.

My special thanks are due to Antonia for reading this book at every stage, administering exactly the right amount of praise and criticism and seeing it most effectively through the press.

Of my husband, who has helped me unstintingly throughout, I shall only say that in every sense without him this family, and hence this book, could not have existed.

Finally, I return to you, my fellow parents, who with your letters and postcards have contributed any spice of real life there may be in the chapters that follow. Each time I open one of these letters I am more than ever impressed by your determination to give your children the best possible chance in life. The spectacle of your humour, patience and absorbed interest convinces me that the art of family life is not dead. In countless homes it is being studied and practised every bit as devotedly as it was in the past. I hope this book will help you.

We shall never discover a better way of living than in families. And you, who are trying to make family life work in these difficult times, deserve all the help we can give you. The traffic, of course, will not be all one way. I, too, have been helped. For every parent has his own or her own golden touch; a magical power to convey some new aspect of what Elizabeth Barrett Browning called 'home-talk and blessing'. To all of you I send a grateful salutation.

Elizabeth Pakenham
April 1954

1

In Praise of Children

'It gave us all a good laugh!' That is the familiar phrase in which parents remember some incidents in the happiest days of their lives, the days when there were children in the home. Children up to mischief, in trouble; doing amazing, amusing, charming, embarrassing, endearing things. That particular episode may have stuck in the memory because of its more than usual outrageousness. All the same, there still comes the cheerful summing-up: 'Anyway, it gave us a good laugh …'

Children's Sayings

With a child in the house—or even next door—you need never have a humourless moment. Think of those wise-cracks! Of the almost professional slickness with which the smallest child answers back. A small girl uses the word 'What?' Her mother looks at her reprovingly and she promptly explains, 'The "Beg your pardon" is tired, but the "What?" is not.'

Even when caught red-handed the little smart-alec defends himself with consummate logic and brevity. A four-year-old boy is told to wash his face after breakfast. He picks up the flannel and thinking he is not observed, just dabs his mouth. 'That's not the way to wash,' says mother, who had been watching after all. 'That was the only part I used,' says he.

Not all wise-cracks are consciously smart. Children misunderstand or mishear worlds. But the results, for us, are often felicitous. A fourteen-year-old schoolgirl, when looking through a song book, came across 'Should Auld Acquaintance'. In amazement she exclaimed, 'Well, I always thought it was "Should All the Quaint 'uns be Forgot!"'

Children with a taste for long words and literary phrases most often make these pleasant mistakes. Antonia, at the age of ten, wanted to call a boy at her school an 'infant prodigy'. 'He's an "infernal reptile",' she brought out with emphasis. A Shakespearean villain 'soliloquising' on the stage was described by her as a 'solo-Quisling'. We still use that expressive word. Rachel, trying to make a good impression on her older brothers and sisters at tea one day, remarked sagely, 'Of course the best part of a lettuce is its "tummy".'

Then there are those *gaffes*. No one has ever discovered how to handle the worst of them—perhaps that 'good laugh' is the only possible solution. But the mild ones certainly cheer us on our way. A little girl had often seen her mother put broken eggs on one side to use in cakes. One day she watched a neighbour open an egg that was bad and throw it away. 'My Mummy always puts the bad eggs in the cakes,' was her comment. My third son Michael was fond of telling new friends that he was born 'on Mummy's wedding day—November 3rd'.

Children Are So Helpful

However the *enfant terrible* often intends to be a ministering angel. There is something irresistible about the child who says 'Let me help'. But what devastating—and comic—things can happen when he sets about it! A three-year-old was very busy on the stairs, 'What are you doing?' called his mother. 'Only just helping you,' came the answer. He was scrubbing the stairs with half a pound of lard.

There is nothing small children love more than 'helping Mummy and Daddy'. We must be prepared to receive their help with heroic fortitude. How would you like your son to announce: 'I've posted your letters all by myself, Mummy'—and then find he had posted them down the drain?

The garden is a favourite place for these exploits. One helpful son watched his father thinning out the parsnips. Later that day he brought indoors all the parsnips that remained. This was called 'weeding Daddy's garden'. A two-year-old pulled up a hundred young cabbages that had just been planted out and laid each neatly by its hole, just as they had been before planting.

A mother, waiting impatiently for the grocer to bring some cooking apples, was presented with the whole of her husband's precious crop of green tomatoes: 'Me grocer man, Mummy. Bring you lots of apples.'

Sometimes children are inspired to beautify their parents' gardens —with fatal results. One little boy reset the shallots upside down, 'because they are prettier that way'. Another horrified his mother by picking off all the tulip heads, only to melt her immediately by pointing to the heap with a sigh of admiration—'Booful, Mum!'

A third spent a busy morning washing the apple trees clean when 'naughty Daddy' had covered them with whitewash. Yet another adorned his father's prize vegetable marrow with a coat of chocolate paint.

Talking of paint, anything connected with mixing, stirring, daubing with brushes, spades or fingers is another favourite way of 'helping'. How I feel for the parents whose son's clothes were ruined by painting their hut as 'a nice surprise'. Or the father who had just laid a cement foundation for his hut, and heard 'an ominous squelching sound'. There was his son digging out the cement much faster than he had laid it.

Yet we must recognise that it is natural and good for children to make a mess with paint, cement or even mud. So give them as many harmless opportunities as possible for 'playing in the dirt', as Hilaire Belloc put it; and if they occasionally seize the wrong chance, try once more to take it with a laugh—as indeed most parents seem to.

Catherine loves 'helping' in my shoe cupboard. When I come to put on a pair in a hurry, I find she has done up every buckle, button, strap and lace beforehand. How I abuse those buttons and bows!

But I must not abuse *her*. For this childish urge to help is valuable. It may not help you, but it helps the child. This may happen in at least three ways.

Helping the Child

1 It teaches him to do things by imitating his parents—however inaccurately.

2 It introduces him to a half-way stage between play and work. When a small girl stands beside her mother on a stool at the sink, apron around waist, arms up to the elbows in lather, what is she doing? 'Playing' or 'working'? Neither, and yet both. At any rate, it is an essential step in her development.

3 It trains her for the time—perhaps ten years hence—when her mother will need her help in the home. In the chapter on 'A Teenager in the Home', we shall see that this help is not always so easy to get. But if a child has happy memories of the sink at three, she may not hate the sight of it so much later on.

I think the account of 'helpful' children I liked best came in a letter from Mrs Lowe, of Cambridge. 'My son John solemnly told a school friend that he and his sister Hope were both born on a Sunday, "because Mum keeps a shop".' The children were delighted to find that even their cat co-operated in the family business. It produced three kittens on a Thursday afternoon—early closing day!

Lastly, what about the children who are not so helpful, either in intention or result? When they eat untidily, drink noisily, interrupt our conversations; combine all the iniquities of Shock-headed Peter, Augustus and Fidgety Phil—can we still praise? At least we can try to keep on smiling as we help them along the road to better things. Sometimes they themselves help us to do so.

Someone told a small girl that it was 'rude to drink with your nose in the cup'. For weeks afterwards this child carefully 'took off' an imaginary nose before a meal and placed it on the table—replacing it later. Picture the consternation in the family when her mother inadvertently threw her 'nose' out of the window with the crumbs for the birds.

Perhaps you feel that this story is too old to be characteristic of any but a few exceptional children? You find it hard to believe such behaviour, even of a child—the most imaginative of God's creatures. But in fact the story is a true one. And it is by no means without parallel. Indeed, nine out of ten children live partly in a world of their own more strange by far than anything we could invent for them. It may be hidden from you. You may not suspect its existence. But it is there. In the next chapter I shall try to enter this world.

To invade the realm of fantasy is to plunge headlong into the child's own inner life. For what is so deeply internal, so utterly part of himself, as a child's imagination? And you will see, as you read on, that the fantasy-theme is never wholly absent from this book. Like a revolving light, it will continue to send its flashes across succeeding problems, illuminating them with a beam at once authentic and direct.

2

The World of Let's Pretend

If you heard that a friend was 'living in two worlds' you would pity him deeply and assume he was mentally ill. Yet our children are doing this very thing every day.

Children generally begin to give us hints of their dream world at about two to three years old. Once while I was staying with a friend I noticed that her small daughter kept hopping off into a corner of the room during breakfast. 'I am laying an egg for your breakfast,' she explained. Altogether about twenty eggs were laid for us.

Animals seem to dominate the dream world of the youngest children. We have all seen that head popping out from under the dining-room table with the words, 'I'm a pussy' or growling that it's a bear or a lion or a tiger. But these familiar examples are nothing to the host of different animals, many with most peculiar names, which children have imagined themselves to be, or to own. I have come across or been told about a frog, a swan, a monkey, a bird, a calf, a sea-lion, a kangaroo, many horses, a pig, a family of squirrels, a mouse, a cow, a panda, a deer, an elephant, innumerable dogs, a guinea-pig, a hippopotamus, 'Mr Cobweb' and his two pigeons, and a bull with the surprising name of 'Polly'.

Between three and five years old the fantasies become extremely elaborate, varied and amusing. As we shall see, they are worth studying for the light they shed on what is going on inside our children's heads.

Fantasy Makes Life Exciting

I was once going up to London for the day when Antonia, then four years old, casually remarked, 'Oh, Tibby and Tello have gone up to London, too.' 'Who are Tibby and Tello?' I asked, properly taken in. 'Just two friends of mine,' was the matter-of-fact reply. 'Tibby' and 'Tello' soon became familiar members of our family circle. They always had a good time, sat up late, went to parties and had lots of new clothes. In fact they led the blissful life of a grown-up in the mind of a four-year-old.

There is no doubt that 'Tibby' and 'Tello' satisfied her own child-ish longing for importance and excitement. They provided what we should call 'vicarious satisfaction'—the satisfaction of our own long-ings and desires through the life of someone else. To a child, the fact that the 'someone else' is purely imaginary matters nothing at all.

My youngest son, Kevin, felt a need, at the tail-end of eight, to bolster up his position in the family. He chose a large grey donkey on wheels—his first Christmas present—on which to build his fantasy. 'Donkey', as he was prosaically called, grew from being an ordinary toy into a kind of superman. He had a birthday every day, was several hundred years old (instead of being the youngest) and had millions of pennies of his own (instead of getting a penny a week). Incidentally, small children become aware of the meaning of money far earlier than we sometimes imagine. They soon discover what an important measuring rod it is in the world of man, and adjust their own ideas accordingly.

The rates of pocket-money throughout the family, and the vari-ous increases that occur with birthdays, cause many an inferiority complex. In one family the children were given a penny a week for every year of their age. 'Oh I shall be glad when I'm a hundred years old!' sighed the youngest. Another 'youngest son' was offered, by a kind uncle, the choice of 'one big penny or two little pennies'. He shocked the elder brothers and sisters by saying without a moment's hesitation. 'Two big pennies.'

But this is a digression. The point about 'Donkey', as about so many other invisible friends whom children invent, was that he lorded it over all the world, just as Kevin longed to do himself. As time went on 'Donkey's' possessions became more and more vast, his empire more far-flung. He came to own racing cars, trains, aeroplanes. We never passed a stately mansion or handsome park without Kevin saying proudly, 'That belongs to Donkey; Donkey lives there ...'

Fantasies Take the Blame

Children use their fantasies, however, for many things besides giving themselves pleasure. They use them as scapegoats, or to save themselves from getting into trouble. One day I told Antonia to put away her dolls and tidy her toy-cupboard. She protested, and as a last resort brought out, 'But I really can't do it! Tibby and Tello simply won't let me. The toy-cupboard belongs to them, and they don't like me interfering with their things.'

On another occasion I came into the drawing-room to find a large vase of flowers upset all over the carpet. Thomas, aged two-and-a-half, was standing by, covered in splashes. 'Oh Thomas,' I exclaimed, 'what a mess you've made!' It was only a matter of seconds before Thomas thought of the answer to that one. 'It wasn't me, Mummy; it was that teddy-bear who did it.' Thomas had always detested soft toys. They seemed to give him the creeps and he would shrink if one was offered him to cuddle. But he found the horrid things had their uses—as scapegoats.

A child who manages occasionally to put a quick one across his parents must be allowed his little victory. It is a great mistake to challenge his world of fantasy with a downright denial of it. 'Of course it wasn't Teddy, it was you,' is quite the wrong answer. It is far better to enter into the game and play it with the child. You can achieve the same results in a better way by saying, 'Well, we must help Teddy to be more careful when he's in Mummy's room, with all her best things around.' The same tactics apply to small children who blame their actual naughtiness or disobedience on some fantasy figure.

It is particularly important not to deny or challenge the child's dream world when he is using it to escape punishment. This is because a certain element of fear is shown to be present by the very fact of his taking refuge in an invented tale. I do not agree with those who say it is bad for older children (or adults) to feel a sense of guilt. But I do think it is bad to make our children feel afraid of telling the truth for fear of punishment. Thus the fantasy is a good way round the difficulty, both for them and for us. It is quite right to accept the child's own explanation, however untruthful it sounds. For you will be helping him to confess *in a symbolic way*, that he has done wrong (if indeed it is wrong, and not just an accident). Beneath the surface of his fantasy there will be tacit agreement between you and him about the true situation. As one parent put it, writing from Edinburgh, 'There's always a natural kind of half-way mark between believing in fantasy and not believing, when the child pretends to believe.' Small children should be allowed to develop naturally out of this stage of half-belief in the world of 'Let's pretend', into the final stage of full belief in the world of reality, without having the process rushed at awkward moments. These awkward moments are so often the ones when they feel afraid and guilty. Their instincts are to dive for cover to the world of make-believe. Do not brutally yank them back into the world of reality.

(These remarks, of course, only apply to small children. I would not for a moment encourage parents to let older children escape from moral decisions with pretence or evasion. Though there are still ways and ways of teaching the moral law to children, whatever their age. But that is another, and a bigger question.)

Study Your Child's Fantasies

At a later stage, say from four to five onwards, the type of fantasy may change again. Children begin to identify themselves with real human beings, instead of mysterious 'friends' and animals. These people are very often the heroes of romance or legend, the cinema or television. A friend's small boy likes to call himself 'Gipsy Boy'. The name 'Gipsy Boy' stands for everything carefree—the freedom and independence that every child longs for. A child who chooses to be a gipsy is giving a big, useful hint to his parents. When you want to give him an outing, take him somewhere where he can climb trees and make a bonfire. Don't dress him up and take him for a walk 'round the shops'.

Fantasies, at whatever stage, can be most helpful to parents trying to understand their children and bring them up in the best way. It is, indeed, impossible to overrate the value of fantasies in this direction. Happy the parent who has a child with an intense gift of imagination! Among other things, a fantasy can show observant parents the secret and otherwise hidden hopes and fears which their child would never consciously reveal to them.

Lindsay, a small boy of three-and-a-half, lived near Derby and had an imaginary friend called 'Bedia' who came to visit him regularly in a horse-drawn cart, from a village twelve miles away. Lindsay's parents noticed that 'Bedia' never stayed for the night, but always had to 'take the horse home to his stable'. In this piece of make-believe Lindsay was clearly revealing his twin and conflicting instincts. One was a longing for freedom from his parents and connection with the wide world. This was represented by the coming of 'Bedia' from twelve miles away. The contrary instinct was to remain in the shelter of his parents' home, and found its expression in 'Bedia's' care never to be caught away from home at night time. But as this instinct was of a fearful nature it had to be concealed and could not even be expressed at one degree from Lindsay himself, e.g. through the feelings of 'Bedia'. It had to be two degrees away, disguised as the horse's need for his stable! Lindsay's parents were wise to take the hint and refrain from trying to push independence upon him too quickly—a course that is particularly tempting to parents of only children who are afraid of mollycoddling and becoming possessive.

I have received a large number of letters which all show in varying but similar ways how a child uses fantasy as a buffer between himself and the growing strains and difficulties of the real world. Take for instance, the rush and hustle of modern transport. We adults are continually aware of the added strain in our lives created by bus queues, crowded platforms at stations, or fast cars. How often do we think of the effect of these things on a child of three or four, who is asked to battle with them several times a week?

A favourite form of defence-mechanism is the imaginery 'friend' or 'family' who gets left behind in the street or off the bus or train. In these cases the child, among other things, is giving his parents a broad hint not to hurry him too much, to go at his slower pace and not at the speed of life as it whirls by in the 20th century.

Here are some examples of this kind of fantasy. From London comes the story of a two-year-old who invented a family of boys called 'Bunna', 'Bourne', 'Dee' and 'Tommy'. 'They had meals and were bathed at the same time as he was,' writes his mother. 'Many a time I have had to recross a busy road because one of the boys had been left behind and would get run over if he crossed alone.'

Now the mother of a three-year-old from Salfrod. 'My little boy used to take out an imaginary "Friend" holding him by the hand. Imagine how I felt when having come out of a shop and carefully crossed the road, my son started to cry because he had left his friend in the shop. I tried to pretend we were still holding Friend's hand, but no. We had to go back across the road to the shop, collect nothing and lead it on our way. Then he was happy again.'

A third instance of the same thing comes from a Sheffield mother. 'Anne, aged three, when accompanying me on walks with her baby brother, always pushed an imaginary pram. One day we called at the grocer's and left the 'pram' outside. As we were returning home she suddenly stopped and said in an anguished tone, 'Oh, Mummy, I've left my pram at the grocer's!' Back we had to go to the spot where she'd left it. She kicked off the 'brake' and rejoined me with a look of intense relief and joy on her face.' One can sympathise with these mothers whose shopping expeditions were thus prolonged by imaginary companions. But one must also admire them for their patience and self-control in not rudely breaking the tiresome fantasy. Later they will reap their reward in happy, well-integrated children.

Bill, aged, three, who led an imaginary bull called 'Polly' around on a real piece of string, showed an interesting variation on this same theme. His mother writes that 'Polly' was a respected member of the family, 'and a great help in making a dreamy three-year-old walk briskly. But try and hurry Bill into a car and inevitably 'Polly' got left out, and the door had to be opened again. I was once reproached with pinching 'Polly's' tail in the door by a too hasty slam.' This story shows that sudden slamming of the car door—as I've always suspected—must frequently take small children by surprise and give them a momentary shock. Bill did not mind being hurried on his feet, but cars were a worry.

Perhaps the most common use of all for an invented 'friend' is to ease the loneliness of an only child. I have had scores of letters describing this type of fantasy, many of them ending with the characteristic comment that the arrival of a baby brother or sister, the beginning of school life, or a visit to the children's ward of a hospital, have provided the real companionship which finally brought the fantasy to an end.

Here is a typical letter from Southport. 'One day as I was preparing dinner in the kitchen Valerie, aged three, said someone was at the front door. I went and opened it, but no one was in sight. I was about to close it when Valerie said, "Oh Mummy, it's Tatterwid and he wants to come in and play with me." So I opened the door again and her face lit up; she looked so pleased. I told her to call him in, which she did. I went back to the kitchen, while she played quite happily in the living-room, showing her new friend all her toys, talking to him all the time. A little while later she came and said, "There's lots more Tatterwids outside who want to come in, Mummy." So once again we trotted to the front door and let them all in. I couldn't help laughing, she was so serious about it all. As time went by these friends visited us frequently and their names were now Begamp, Tempest and Tatterwide. We used to ask what they were like and whether they were all boys, but she would only smile and say they had run down the "grid" (imaginary) behind the settee.

I got worried in the end she was so serious about it, and when asked to do something that didn't please her, she would reply, "Oh, Begamp wouldn't like me to do that!" I mentioned it to the welfare officer who kindly informed me it was quite natural and she was a little lonely. Now she has a two-year-old brother Paul, and Begamp, Tempest and Tatterwid are things of the past.'

3

What Do We Learn from Fantasy?

The reaction of parents to their children's imaginary worlds varies a good deal. At one end of the scale comes an anonymous correspondent who sees in these imaginative children the geniuses of the future—the Whittles, Newtons, Shakespeares, Flemings, Nightingales. He urges parents and others to give their fantasies every possible encouragement, so that the day may never come when he has to sign himself 'Alas No Wonderland'.

At the other end of the scale come the considerable number of parents who are made distinctly uneasy by the intensity of their children's belief in unreality. The letter from Valerie's mother is an example. She was fortunate to have a welfare officer to advise her. Another mother wrote to me whose two daughters were both born cripples. She was disturbed by the fact that they played elaborate games of make-believe up to the ages of seven and nine, always pretending they were Eastern dancers or fairy princesses. She had never heard of the same thing in other children, and feared that her husband was right when he said they were 'cracked in the head like their mother!'

Many parents seem to find the child's fantasy easier to 'take' if there is at least some sign of a concrete object involved, and not just the thinnest of thin air. A letter from Waltham Cross puts this point of view. 'My little girl at two had her own make-believe world and an invisible girl-friend she called Jean. She would always be walking round the room with hand out-stretched, talking to Jean and holding her hand. I worried about it at first, as I have an older boy who never talked to himself. So I bought her a big doll and told her to call the doll Jean. Then she could talk to someone we could all see!'

In actual fact a child's fantasy is equally 'real' or 'unreal', silly or understandable (whichever way you look at it) whether he bases it on a concrete object or on nothing visible at all. It may be less eerie for the parent, but it makes no difference to the child. Some children like something visible to hitch it on to; others do not. Kevin had a toy donkey, Antonia had nothing. On the whole I have found it is more common to have nothing. And when a real object is used it is generally of the more sketchy and symbolic kind. One child pulled along a stalk of real grass, at the end of which was Fido an imaginary dog. (Fido would lie under the bus seat and cause great embarrassment when he was told to keep still, for the conductor would then come up and ask for his fare!).

Another child, who longed for a companion, invented a girl-friend who was sometimes embodied in the visible form of her mother's mop. 'She would borrow my mop, turn it upside down and gently twist or shake it, to give the illusion of hair on a taller girl, and she would hold extensive conversations with this friend.'

But I believe that most children hesitate to allow any real object to form an integral part of their make-believe world. For they are always afraid lest the real world should break into the world of imagination, and once given a chance, destroy it.

This view is strengthened by the considerable number of children who complain that their parents tread on, sit upon and even occasionally squash to death their imaginary friend. Surely this is symbolic of the child's persistent fear of the real world's destructive effect on his imaginary one. And of course it is mainly through the parents that the unwelcome world of reality is most vigorously thrust upon him. Here are four characteristic examples of fear for a fantasy's safety being symbolically expressed.

1 'My son aged three much admired an older boy named Reg, but owing to the difference in age had not many opportunities of playing with him. So he invented a friend called Tender Rench (his pronunciation of Pretend Reg). One day as I was washing his face

he suddenly burst into tears, and told me I had trodden on Tender Rench who was standing beside him.'

2 A little girl was happily pushing her doll's pram in the garden. Suddenly she began sobbing. Her mother ran out and was told between sobs that the child's sister—just come home from school—had trodden on *my husband*. The sister jumped back, only to be met with more shrieks: 'Oh, now you have trodden on my little girl!'

3 During a bus ride a small boy warned his cousin 'not to stand on Tiny-One's tail'—Tiny-One being his imaginary dog. The older cousin did of course unwittingly stand on it, and was told angrily and loudly to move. 'To restore order,' writes the mother, 'my brother-in-law had to tell his own son in a loud voice to "get off Tiny-One's tail". Other passengers were craning for a glimpse of the dog, and obviously thinking that they were in the company of a party on parole from an asylum.' Buses seem to be the places where the real and the imaginary worlds have their worst clashes, and cause most embarrassment.

4 The last example comes from Bristol. 'When my daughter Pamela was very small she had an imaginary friend called Pomona. Many a time we have started out on a walk, when Pamela would run back, stand on the corner for a few minutes, and then say, "Mummy, wait for Pomona". Or, on seating myself in a bus, Pamela would exclaim, with a stricken look on her face, "Not there, Mummy, you are sitting on Pomona!"'

How Do Fantasies End?

People who have never had experience of these fantasies may be curious to know how they come to an end—or do they continue in changing forms for ever, preventing the adolescent, and finally even the adult, from coming to grips with real life?

The answer is that these fantasies normally come to an end around five or six years old (often with the beginning of school) but their actual 'ends' are as various and fascinating as the fantasies themselves.

Sometimes the end is highly dramatic and sudden, sometimes it is a gradual disappearance. Here are two examples of the dramatic type from different children. An imaginary Aunt 'was bending down to get coal and lightning struck her'. And an imaginary boy called Goeffrey 'died in the night from blood pressure'. This news was suddenly announced at breakfast.

Other favourite ways of getting rid of a no-longer-needed fantasy are to say, 'He's left the country', or 'They've gone abroad'; and alas, most popular of all, 'He got run over'.

One acute mother realised that her daughter was desperately trying to get rid of an imaginary guinea-pig when she started crying one day and saying it had fallen down a grating. 'She refused to leave it and seemed so upset that much to the amusement of the passers-by I had to kneel down on the pavement and pretend to rescue it. Soon after this we bought her a real kitten and "guinea-pig" was allowed to die a natural death.'

A particularly interesting letter shows a child actually accusing his parents of destroying his imaginary world, and the parents rejoicing over its end. 'My little son had an imaginary mouse called Twinks. This mouse was always on the pillow waiting for him when he went to bed, and it was always sitting beside him when he bathed. If he had been away from home, his first act on returning would be to rush to the cupboard where Twinks lived and make a great fuss of him. But the poor little imaginary mouse was killed when my husband rushed downstairs one morning and accidentally trod on him. He was gathered up with floods of tears and tenderly buried in the garden. My son's grief was shattering, and was fast getting us to believe in the mouse. As a family, we were all relieved when Twinks departed this life.' However, in most cases these invented friends bring nothing but happiness into their creator's lives, and the whole family usually regrets their eventual disappearance.

It is interesting to observe that children often choose to recognise their fantasy-object, or deliberately identify it for the first time with some real thing, at the very moment when they are on the point of getting rid of it for ever. In other words, at the place where the paths of the real and unreal world meet, the unreal one is obliterated. These moments correspond to the striking of the clock in *Cinderella*, and the fatal gazing at the real Sir Lancelot by the Lady of Shalott, instead of looking only at his image in the mirror.

I quote two examples of this kind of recognition, which destroys the fantasy. A four-year-old boy invented a magical black cat, known as My Cat. This cat lasted for eighteen months, until one day the child saw a real black cat in the garden. 'He was very excited,' says his mother, 'and came running out of the house crying "Here is My Cat!" But he could not catch the animal. And that was the last we ever heard of My Cat.'

A father from Thaxted, Essex, describes how his son's fantasy came to an end when he tried to communicate it to his father—an adult. The boy often used to disappear to a country called Double Dess, which was 'just beyond Africa'. One day this four-year-old asked his father if he, too, would like to go there. His father tells the sad story of the expedition. 'It was a long walk along country lanes. He kept saying anxiously, "It's not far now." We came to a village. "It's here," he said. "Just over there." Then he said sadly, "You can't see it, can you, Daddy? That's because it's magic and it vanishes when grown-ups come." I pretended I could see it but he was not deceived. He never spoke of Double Dess again.'

A third story, this time from Burnley, shows the reverse side of the penny—a child steadily refusing to recognise or point out the position of his fantasy in the real world, because he knows that if he does so he will destroy it. 'When my eldest son was three he often visited a mysterious shop named Breakanarrys. It was a marvellous shop and sold everything under the sun from sweets to motor-cars, and, most endearing of all, Breakanarrys never asked for payment. At home he chatted freely about it; knew exactly where it was situated, "just down the road next to So-and-So's". But when out with me nothing would induce him to speak of it or point it out.'

The Borderline Stage

When the child is allowed to develop gradually and naturally from pure fantasy into realms approaching nearer and nearer to real life, it is possible and illuminating to distinguish the various stages between the two extremes through which he passes. For there are many intermediate stages between absolute, intense belief in fantasy, and utter rejection and disbelief in it. Kevin at the age of six is a matter-of-fact schoolboy when he is playing with his friends. His baby world of make-believe seems miles away. But when he is alone he often likes to step just over the border, into a game where illusion and reality are separate, and yet mingled. The other day he was playing in my bedroom and I noticed that a tremendous duel had begun to develop in my long mirror. He danced about in front of the mirror with an imaginary gun in his hand, making horrific faces and shouting 'Who are you? I want to know who you are … Bang! Bang! You dare do that to me …' At last he fell to the ground with a groan, rolled over, sat up and exclaimed in a voice of comic despair and surprise, 'Heavens! I've shot myself!'

The most impressive example I have come across of a child actually putting into his own words the transition from childish fantasy to almost adult imagination, comes from the mother of a boy of only five. 'My son said to me, "What makes you think you are here?" "Because I am walking on the terrace with you admiring the roses," I answered. "But if you chose to be in Bournemouth, then you could be there," said he. "No," I replied, "because then I should see the sea and not the roses." His answer was, "You can see what you choose to see, and I choose to be in Bournemouth and I can see the sea. You can always see what you choose to see."'

When we find children of only five years old capable of making such profound observations, we should indeed be chary of planting our big clumsy feet in their imaginary worlds—worlds that are as delicate as gossamer, yet at the time as real to the child as the truth.

Parents sometimes feel they ought to break up these daydreams for fear of the child growing up in a permanent state of self-deception, or even of deliberate untruthfulness and dishonesty. If those parents realised how common such fantasies are, and what an important part they play in the child's development, they would cease to worry. Instead they would study them with immense interest (and often great amusement) learning from them some of the most important secrets of their children's inner life. And in speaking of them to the children themselves, they would treat the fantasy with exactly the same matter-of-course acceptance as the children do—not being too curious, nor yet too indifferent.

Children have the priceless gift of a perfectly normal and perfectly healthy 'split personality'. With absolute ease they can both believe and disbelieve in the same thing. They can be two different people at the same time. And to crown it all, they can clothe their dream world in words so strange, mysterious and expressive that one readily agrees all children are poets at heart.

Where do their names come from—those queer fantastic folk of the land of make believe? Syffel and Mrs Dabbidas, Pollina and Vesina Metropole, Begamp and Tatterwid. Those innumerable sets of twins, too, surely the blood brothers and sisters of tweedledum and Tweedledee: Quiddy and Quoddy, Forms and Fimes, Mrs Bonzing and Mrs Sparing, Miss Booty and Miss Pincher.[1]

Evidently they come from a place where language, like all else, sparkles with the vitality of poetic fancy. It is a magical place, at once secret and exposed to prying eyes. As parents, we have it in our power to double its gifts to our fortunate children who hold the key and can live there during two or three happy years. For by our own tact and skill, by sympathy tempered with care never to intrude, we can give them the chance to carry much of its magic over into the sober world that lies ahead.

Note

1 These names (and many others like them) are all taken from parents' letters.

4

Can We End those Quarrels?

I suppose that to us parents, if the most attractive thing about children is their imagination, the least attractive is their quarrels. But we must try not to let those whines and moans (so much more irritating than downright roars) get too much on our nerves. Children take quarrelling in their stride, especially young children. And they are the ones who do it most. It's all part of their day's work. It is a form of exciting activity for them.

It angers them, amuses them, stretches their mental—and physical!—powers to the full. During a quarrel they feel intensely alive. Vanished is even the whiff of boredom. And boredom, not quarrelling, is the real enemy of a happy childhood.

But now look at the parents' point of view. I can think of at least six good reasons why I dislike quarrelling. Every other parent can think of a few more.

1 It represents the difference between war and peace in the family.
2 It interrupts my work.
3 It is ugly to hear and see.
4 My husband, like all fathers, hates it. Away from home a good deal of the time, as fathers must be, he likes to think of his family as a haven of tranquillity. Quarrelling destroys that picture.
5 We both feel guilty when our children fight. After all, we have provided them with the heredity and environment for their quarrels.
6 It is our responsibility to find ways of stopping it.

Punishment is sometimes necessary. My own parents had effective but opposite methods of dealing with quarrelsome children. My father always automatically punished the child who was howling. My mother on the other hand unhesitatingly punished the one who was not! She assumed, probably rightly, that it had caused the trouble.

We children recognised this as a kind of rough justice. It was all in the luck of the game whether father or mother caught you quarrelling. Certainly such simple and direct methods are far better than the parents joining in the argument, and making desperate and angry efforts to get to the bottom of it. This may seem fairer, but in fact it usually only results in adding to the hullabaloo. The quarrellers secretly enjoy the heightened drama of parental intervention. They plead their own cause with growing excitement and enthusiasm. Instead of subsiding, the heat of battle intensifies.

Punishments and Rewards

The obvious procedure for parents is to settle disputes with the minimum fuss and maximum speed. Turn the children's attention away as soon as possible to some new subject. A quick suggestion for another game or activity makes a more satisfactory end to a quarrel than a long drawn-out family court-scene, with father or mother as judge.

Apart from punishment, which I shall discuss in more detail in a later chapter, how can we prevent quarrelling? Personally I believe judicious bribery has its uses.

Bribery, of course, may be a dangerous weapon. Children who are always bribed to be good may never learn to be good without it. This would be a sorry state of affairs. And a serious dereliction of duty on the part of parents. For it is the duty of parents to train their children in moral sense. That is, in knowing the difference between right and wrong. Not just between nice and nasty, pleasant and unpleasant. When a child realises that difference, he will understand what it is to do a good thing for its own sake.

Once that foundation is laid at home, the child will go through life loving things for their own sakes. And there lies the secret of happiness. He will love learning and knowledge for its own sake. He will do a good job for its own sake. He will love his wife for her own sake, not just for the comfort or pleasure she gives him. So—to return to the prevention of quarrelling—we certainly don't want to lay the foundations of good behaviour in bribery.

But small rewards need not be banned from the process of training. One extremely 'advanced' educationist, Mr A.S. Neill, well-known Headmaster of Summerhill School, describes in his book, *The Free Child*, how he had to pay the children to wheel away barrowfuls of earth. Without payment they groused; with pay they did it happily. Mr Neill seems a little unhappy himself about this procedure, but accepts it as one of the facts of life.

Some parents always give their children small 'bribes' for doing odd jobs about the house and garden. I fell into this habit myself after the Boy Scouts' 'Bob-a-job' week in our village—an entirely praiseworthy affair. But when the 'week' was over Michael and Kevin thought it a pity to drop such a good idea. So for a time it was pennies for everything: 6d each for polishing the car, 2d for picking off 50 dandelion heads (it had to be raised to 200, there were so many!), 3d for finding my lost secateurs. Finally I struck when Kevin offered to fetch me the trowel from the toolshed, adding in all good faith: 'How much will that be, Mummy? Sevenpence halfpenny?'

There are certain emergencies when some kind of bribery seems the best solution. It is a wet afternoon. You have visitors. The children must play on their own. And they must not quarrel. The promise of a treat 'if you are good the whole afternoon' is a sure way of preventing quarrels.

Children's quarrels can be divided into two kinds: Sudden flare-ups and permanent maladjustments. If two of your children are always at loggerheads this probably means they are temperamentily incompatible. The only thing to do is to keep them as separate as possible—separate bedrooms, separate schools. It is often difficult to arrange, but it is well worth the inconvenience. For these children can become friends in time, provided their memories of youthful antagonism are not too vivid and numerous.

If, however, your children's quarrels are really flare-ups of temper, happening between any of the children and not always the same pair, then my advice is: Don't worry. This applies especially to the parents of four or more children. Quarrelling is the occupational disease of large families.

Parents' Quarrels

I may seem to have made rather light of children's dogfights. Parents' open quarrelling, on the other hand, is the supreme offence against family life. A quarrel in front of the children makes an indelible and terrifying impression on the child's mind. Child psychologists often trace stammering in a child to the time when he first heard his parents quarrelling.

While I was writing this chapter Antonia recalled to me an incident which I had entirely forgotten, but which she and Thomas had remembered for fifteen years.

Apparently my husband and I had some argument about their bedtime which ended in my saying, 'If that's how you feel, you can put them to bed yourself,' and I launched the telephone directory at his head. Our two horrified children marched upstairs and hid in a corner of their bedroom. They were convinced we were on the point of divorce—not because we were always quarrelling, but just because we never quarrelled in front of them at all!

For it is a curious fact that parents who hardly ever quarrel seem to upset their children more on the rare occasions when they do so, than those who have continual rows. One of my daughters commented the other day on a girl-friend's amazing attitude. 'She tells me stories every day about her mother's and father's quarrels, and how her granny eggs her mother on. She doesn't seem to mind a bit and just laughs.'

True, the child doesn't seem to mind. She is forced to make light of the situation. Children are adept at making a virtue of necessity. We all know the child of divorced parents who boasts, 'I've got two Mummies and two Daddies!' The child grows a kind of defensive shell. But the real hurt is deep and all-pervasive. It may even damage his sense of security so badly that he in turn is not able to make a happy marriage. The moral is clear. Parents, if you must spar, let it not be in front of the children. Remember, there are times of stress when Mrs Grundy's discarded slogan, *pas devant les enfants*, still applies.

Quarrelling Among Friends

So far I have only considered quarrelling within a family. Some people may feel this is the worst kind of quarrelling, just as civil war is generally thought to be a more horrible kind of war than war between different nations. But we must face the fact that in one sense family quarrels are easier to cope with than other kinds. At least you can deal with your own children as you think fit. You can adopt any method of prevention you like. You can punish the guilty ones. It's all 'in the family'.

But what happens when your child scraps with her friend from next door? The holidays are here. Your children miss their school-friends. They invite them round. So they come to play—and stop to quarrel. When you hear the regular slanging-match begin, what sort of line should you take? 'I am delighted to think that the great art of insult is not yet quite dead.' So spoke one popular exponent, Gilbert Harding. But I wonder how many harassed mothers take this robust view.

Here is a letter which went straight to my heart. 'How can we deal with our children's quarrels with their friends? I was at my wits' end after the long school holidays. I am always fair if my daughter is wrong. I will say so and punish her. But not so the other mothers. Of course I do not blame other children, I treat them with kindness and listen to their story. My child is twelve, the other two a few years older.'

This mother pin-points a tricky problem—how to correct other people's children. Children who cannot get on with their friends have not the same excuse as quarrelsome brothers and sisters. Families do not choose each other. But friends do. So it is up to them not to behave like rival canvassers at an election, or bargain-hungry women at a sale. Here are some suggestions for parents who will have to tackle this situation next holidays.

Put the facts bluntly to your own child first. 'You have chosen these children for your friends. Presumably because you like them. If you don't really like them, choose others. No one minds occasional scraps. But this incessant bickering doesn't sound like true friendship at all.'

If your child is really fond of her friends she will heed your warning. She will see the logic of your complaint. But if her so-called friends are just a habit—children she has not chosen but casually accepted because they are neighbours—she will abandon them with relief. Of course you must now help her to find others more compatible. In some cases children are not really as free to make the friends of their choice as we suppose. Sometimes questions of neighbourhood and distance may choose their friends for them, just as chance chooses their brothers and sisters. So when quarrelling breaks out too often between next-door neighbours, make a great effort and ask a real friend, if need be from a distance. This will mean entertaining and feeding the visitor for a whole day. But it will be worth it, in peace and quiet.

Be Fair

But suppose the warning is effective and the neighbourly quarrelling decreases. Even so, it may still break out occasionally. The next thing is to make sure you are scrupulously fair, if you decide to intervene. This is particularly important with older children. The great thing with younger children, as we saw above, is to settle the trouble as quickly as possible, without going too deeply into the rights and wrongs of it. But children nearing their teens have a keen interest in justice and fair play. They can understand a logical argument. Nor can their attention be so easily switched from the subject of the quarrel to some new idea.

Scrupulous fairness applies to your own child, as well as to the visitor. Conscientious parents are apt to be over-severe with their own children, for fear of seeming to favour them. A Brighton mother writes how she punished her seven-year-old son for quarrelling with his little cousin, who was paying them a visit. She sent him supperless to bed and took the visitor out for a bus ride, as a treat. When they got home she found a piece of paper hung on a string across the hall. On it was printed, 'Dear Mummie, the thief on the cross was forgiven, so won't you forgive your boy and let him down to supper?'

When both are to blame it does more harm than good to punish one's own child and not the visitor. The child who is punished feels doubly irritated with the child who is not. Almost certainly the result will be more quarrelling, not less.

It is not always so difficult to correct other people's children as it seems. So long as the 'other child' sees you are treating all alike. Judith, at twelve, was questioned by me on this point. She admitted that being scolded by someone else's mother was quite reasonable, if one deserved it. On the other hand, she insisted that very few mothers ever dared to do it; and when they did, it was rather embarrassing!

On the whole, I believe most children will accept anything that is fair. Children have an almost over-developed sense of fair play. 'It's not fair... It's quite fair... You're being so unfair...' Sometimes I really detest that word. But despite its occasional misuse the word 'fair' still remains the parent's guide and friend.

But though most children will accept what seems fair treatment without complaint, this does not apply to all. Children who are never disciplined or punished in their own homes may refuse to accept even fair censure from you. How to deal with a really spoilt child—someone else's at that—presents a thorny problem indeed. Personally I see only two ways out. You may have to be quite drastic and decide that a child brought up in a home with ideals and methods so contrary to your own is no fit companion for yours. When our children are reaching adolescence we cannot be casual about their friends.

But of course it is better to influence a child than to ban it. Banning children as 'bad influences' goes against the grain. Particularly when we realise that difficult and aggressive children, who seem to have been spoilt by too much love, are often suffering from too little, or the wrong kind. So let us at least try the other way. Talk the matter over with the parents, for a start. If they are human they will not enjoy the quarrelling either. Call a 'council of peace'. Hammer out joint action. Decide not only on punishments, but treats as a reward for peaceful days. Arrange a rota of visits. Then the quarrelling will not always take place in your house. And that unsuccessful parent, who has hitherto avoided the difficult job of giving her child loving discipline, may at last be goaded into action.

Some children behave better with friends than they do in their own homes. But with others it is just the opposite. Children who are too severely disciplined at home may let off steam when on a visit. A Lancashire mother found her daughter and a playmate barefoot on her kitchen table. 'You wouldn't dance on your mother's table,' said her hostess reproachfully. 'No,' replied the dancer, 'but I'd like to.'

One word of consolation for those who try all prescriptions but find the holiday quarrels still rage. If you feel at your wits end, it is just because the children are on top of you getting on your nerves, instead of being packed off into the street and left to their own devices. Almost certainly you are doing them a great service by having them around, and enduring the disturbances. It's better for children to play at home, under your eye—even quarrelling—than to go off you know not where, with companions you know not of. You may have less peace now. But you are avoiding more trouble later.

5

'I've Got Nothing to Do . . .'

'What shall I do? I don't know what to do.' These words are an alarm signal. Parents ignore them at their peril. For children, like Nature, abhor a vacuum. One moment they have nothing to do. Next, they have found something appalling, like washing down the car 'for a nice surprise!' This brief operation—for it only takes ten minutes, and they are soon saying 'What shall we do next?'—has involved the ruin of two hand-towels, the emptying of your tin of polish, scratches on the paint and the necessity for an immediate re-wash. So it is worth laying plans for the 'what shall we do?' campaign these holidays.

(Incidentally, washing the car can be quite a useful occupation, provided it is not done 'as a surprise' but under some sort of direction, either of a parent or older child. Michael, Catherine and Kevin have learnt to do it very well for me. I usually pay them something, as long as they refrain from hosing each other and getting the chromium polish on to the paint.)

The trouble about the Christmas holidays is that so much has to be done indoors. Of course the Christmas cards may be right, as they are once in a quarter of a century. It may be a white holiday, and no child asks what to do while the snow lasts. But how shall we keep them busy if, as is more the likely, the house is full of drying macs and Wellingtons and bored children?

Dressing-Up

My first choice for the Christmas holidays is dressing-up. I've yet to find the child of any age who did not succumb to this enchantment. It seems odd that they should, when you first come to think of it. After all, children have hardly begun to discover their own personalities. They are busy trying to find out who and what they are. Yet one of their favourite games is dressing-up as someone else. Perhaps dressing-up is itself part of this business of self-exploitation. The child gradually discovers himself by disguising himself as another person or thing.

An anecdote from Coventry tells how the parents of a small girl lost her one afternoon, and after a fruitless search finally decided to go down the road and enlist the help of a neighbour. On their way they passed a group of children who had been playing for some time nearby. 'Suddenly a small voice said "Hullo, Daddy!" There she was, all dressed up in someone else's clothes! We had watched these children playing, but failed to recognise our own daughter.'

Even teenagers are not above dressing-up. They may be encouraged to write and produce a simple play or charade suitable to the season or occasion. Judith, at thirteen, produced a Nativity play called 'Silent Night?' The question mark in the title was to suggest that Satan and his fallen angels had been noisy and active on that night two thousand years ago, and had made a determined attempt to kidnap the Babe, an attempt which would undoubtedly have been successful but for the presence of mind of the archangel Michael.

Smaller children are happiest in a variety show. Each child performs the act it likes best. Some are singers, some ballet dancers, some reciters, some comedians. The youngest can be what Shakespeare called 'tumblers'. A friend of ours, a farmer's son of twelve, has a wonderful whistling act composed of the notes of wild birds. An older and a younger boy can do a very successful ventriloquist-and-dummy scene together.

One Christmas we had a mock circus—half the children being animals and the rest clowns and acrobats. Luckily no one had yet seen the man shot out of the gun.

A four-year-old from Bedlington, Northumberland, at once reproduced his first visit to a circus for his parents. 'We must all sit holding our imaginary programmes,' writes his mother, 'while he does all the tricks we have already seen. The funniest is to see him walking round with his head tilted back and a ball on his forehead, imitating the sea-lion. After a time he gets up on a chair, still holding the ball, for the final act. Then we must all applaud. Finis.'

The success of dressing-up and acting depends on two things. First, an audience of patient parents. This is often no small sacrifice. Intervals are unduly long. Older actors get the giggles; young ones become tongue-tied. When the end comes at long last, you must give unadulterated applause. If you have some dramatic criticism to offer it is best to wait until the children's excitement and effort have subsided. On no account must you damp their ardour at the time of the performance.

But if you can train yourself to be a perfect audience, what a reward is in store! The children will spend happy hours preparing for the great day. They will devise curtains, a stage, tickets, programmes and even refreshments. One word of warning. Brothers must not be pressed into the cast against their will. All but a few boys are natural wreckers of home theatricals. If, on the other hand, they come in voluntarily, success is assured.

The other essential is a good 'acting-box'. I have stored mine with treasures of footwear and clothing over a period of twenty years. Everything is grist to the mill. Great-Aunt's wasp-waisted riding-habit and exquisite fichus and capes. Great-Uncle's walking-stick, Grandfather's plume and breastplate, someone's B.A. gown trimmed with rabbit-fur, and everybody's cast-off finery from 1854 to 1954 inclusive. People who keep chickens always find a good use for scraps. The family acting-box does the same for wearing apparel. Apart from old evening dresses, the most valuable trophies are uniforms of all kinds and top-hats. Jumble sales are helpful in the hat line. Last holidays we acquired a splendid bowler and four felts—all for 6d.

But towards the end of the holidays your children may begin to feel they know all the acting-clothes by heart. Now is the moment to open your own wardrobe—gingerly but generously. To dress up in a grown-up's real clothes is the height of bliss. A letter comes from Ross, Lancashire: 'My favourite dream was to dress up like my elder sister. The effort of tottering around on high heels and wearing smart fancy hats made my feet ache and my head dizzy. But now that I can wear those three-inch heels and any hat I choose, the pleasure I got then and still get from those childish pleasures, far outdoes the real thing.'

Experimental hair-dressing will also keep children busy for hours. Never throw away a bridesmaid's wreath or old-fashioned hair comb. One of our prized possessions is a 'tail' of hair cut off when I was eighteen. Another word of warning, however. Children are sometimes tempted to make permanent transformations in their hair. One correspondent remembers a fair-haired twin treating her hair with black boot-polish. 'We were all convinced in the family that this twin was never again quite so fair as the other!' Judith at five cut a large bite out of her fringe the day she was going to be photographed. A mother writing from Kent says she discovered her son 'standing in front of the long mirror cutting his hair off. "I wanted to look like Mr X" he explained, mentioning a friend of ours who was bald. Needless to say we were amused, but it took a very long time to get his hair normal again.' So take heart, fathers who are thinning on top. You are not without your admirers.

I'm afraid dressing-up has one drawback. It sometimes promotes quarrels instead of preventing them. A gold and jewelled collar I once wore as Queen Eleanor in a pageant proved a terrible apple of discord. Luckily a rival to the collar appeared on the scene shortly afterwards, in the form of a pair of long black silk stockings. (Children's tastes are unaccountable.) The solution, of course, is to insist on the children taking turns. If they still quarrel over one particular treasure, remove it altogether. Put it into a 'museum case' to be admired at a distance.

If you are thinking of presents and want to make cheap additions to your acting-box, I suggest two winners. Masks, from any good toyshop. Make-up sets—the very best never more than a few shillings.

Building a New World

And now that all the equipment is collected, what shall we do with it? Nothing is more popular with children than building a house inside your house—a small world of their own within the world they know. You've got to make up your mind to one thing, of course. The children will turn everything upside down. Perhaps that is the only way to make a new world. Not only that, but they will continually be adding to the chaos, as long as the game lasts. How often have I caught myself saying, 'Can't you begin playing with your house now, instead of bringing in more and more things?'—cushions from all over the house, bedspreads, deck-chairs.

The answer is that the game itself consists in the making, adding, increasing. For every ten minutes a child spends playing in the completed edifice, he will spend half an hour building it. I have known children spend hours on elaborate structures, and then never play with them at all.

Another point is tidying up afterwards. On principle, you should make them tidy away at least part of it at the end of the game. But children, unlike some adults, find it easier and more congenial to create than to destroy. Clearing up their great edifices is really painful to them as well as being infinitely tedious. So be merciful in the token tidying you insist on them doing. And if you have time, lend a hand in the process yourself. That seems to make the operation much more palatable. If you let the burden of tidying up hang too heavily over them during the creative period, you may end up by stifling all desire to play these imaginative, but dislocating games. Such a result would damage their natural development. It would also deprive you of one of the best ways of keeping them happy on a wet day.

Let us assume, then, that you have brought yourself to allow the children to turn one room completely upside down. And there has not been too much gloomy talk on the lines of, 'Now don't forget you've got to tidy it all away afterwards.' The new world will now come into glorious being. A boat, bus, train, aeroplane, shop, post office, bank, desert island, school, orchestra, hospital, holiday camp—

all these have been made by my children at one time or other—even, as one mother discovered to her horror, in a cemetery.

'My son decided he would be a grave-digger, and staged elaborate ceremonies in the parlour. Staggering in with a box on his shoulder, Peter buried it with cushions on the couch, after a short reading from the nearest book. I found the atmosphere very depressing. Wreaths of wild flowers on the mantelpiece, black-edged cards and Peter was wearing a black arm-band.'

Peter, as one might have guessed, lived opposite a cemetery, hence his acute observation of what to him was a subject of intense factual interest, not in the least lugubrious or morbid. His behaviour was as innocent as that of the children in the French film *The Secret Game*. But on the whole, children's worlds seem to be divided between the spheres of travel, adventure and everday life. Here is the living-room of a house in Leamington Spa, turned into a shopping centre. 'Each corner represented a shop to my three small sons. This was during the war, when strict rationing was in progress. Before each meal out would come the shopping basket and ration books. They would consult each other as to what they would like best to eat: then into the corner shop they would go and buy everything they most desired. The post office was in the centre of the table. Here you just scribbled on a piece of paper, and you could get all the money you wanted to buy the things. Needless to say, we had the most wonderful meals.'

A mother of four, writing from R.A.F. Married Quarters at Chester, describes how her three-year-old twins turned a wet afternoon into a country picnic. 'I heard them go off in a car for a picnic, all make-believe, of course. The twins decided that their seven-year-old sister must be a dog, so she duly got down on all fours and joined in the game. Next the twins asked me for some tit-bits to eat on the picnic, which I gave them on three small plates. Off they trotted to get spoons, but when the dog asked for a spoon, "Oh no!" they said, "eat with your mouth." And she had to, kneeling on the floor with her head to the plate.'

An Oldham mother sends an ingenious recipe for turning washing-day into a concert. 'My daughters, one four-and-a-half, the other two-and-a-half, had a small stool each. I used to put on them two rows of washing-pegs, and they called it "playing the piano". It certainly kept them quiet for a good hour, especially on washing-day.'

Sometimes the itch to turn the room upside down goes too far. Mrs Dedman from Bishop's Stortford discovered her daughter's bedroom a shambles. 'Every drawer open and the contents strewn about. "Have you been in Diana's room?" I asked Eric, aged seven. He hung his head, rolled his eyes and a grin flashed across his face. "I've been pretending there's been a burglar!" he confessed.'

Some imaginative children find even one piece of furniture enough to form the basis of their 'world within a world'. They manage to turn it into a complete home, as a robin does with a flower-pot or saucepan. A mother from Mansfield, Notts., found her four-year-old son imitating the habits of both the robin and the jackdaw. 'During the process of decorating, a large upholstered chair was deposited on its side in the hall. After a few days the increasing disappearance of odd articles became more than coincidence. So I accused my son of hiding them, and was told with great pride that "Merrygrin has taken them to Roundtree Castle for the Coronation". A search in the upturned chair revealed a velvet cushion, a teddy-bear, a pair of scissors, a cake-tin, four spoons and two forks, a pigeon's feather, an eggcup full of water with daisies in it and numerous strips of coloured material. This had been pinned from one side of Roundtree Castle to the other, like streamers. Merrygrin, I was told, is invisible to grown-ups, which accounts for the articles' quiet going.'

Of all my family's imaginative games I think the orchestra surprised me most, as no more unmusical family than ours can exist. But one day Michael (9), Catherine (7), and Kevin (5), began collecting small objects of all kinds and making them into various musical instruments. They spent a great deal of time in drawing elaborate scores for each instrument. In fact it was fortunate for the rest of the family that the making of the orchestra took so long there was little time left for the actual playing.

Active Games Indoors

Older children need active games indoors to let off steam. If you have a big room, 'Going round the room without touching the floor' is unbeatable. Old newspapers make more economical stepping-stones than one's best cushions. A friend tells me they used to play this game as children all over the house—which would solve the problem of the big room.

A quiet yet active game for the evening is creeping from one dark part of the house to another, without being caught. It's name, I am told, is 'Devil in the Dark'. Then there's the old favourite 'Murder'. This also is played mostly in the dark, with detective and murderer drawn from the same number of turned-down cards as there are children in the game. The detective remains outside the room while the murder is committed in the dark. Lights are then turned up and he questions all present. Truthful answers are demanded from all—except the murderer. From his logical powers the detective then deduces who is the villain.

Warning! Do not invite Granny to play! Ours found it much too realistic and did not sleep well that night.

For a special treat try 'Rescue' all over the house. This is the noisiest of all games, but it can be played by children of all ages, and does not need darkness.

Paper Games

How about running a family newspaper? This lasts the whole holidays, and all take a hand. Judith at thirteen runs one modelled conscientiously on the back pages of all the dailies she is acquainted with. No feature is forgotten. There is Mrs Darlington Pity's Distress Column: 'Question: I get nightmares. What shall I do? Answer: Stay awake all night, dear.' Beauty Hints included 'Smear your nails with pink toothpaste and rub hard. This should produce a clean shining toe.' A popular feature was the crossword, with a polite note printed beneath the clues: 'Please use pencil not ink on the crossword, and rub it out afterwards.' This was because *The Parrot* only ran into one copy. There were numerous ads, some portentously wordy like the 100-word advertisement for a Society called 'Think Inc.' supplied by a philosophical undergraduate from Oxford; others simple and direct, such as 'Take Temper Tablets. They Make You Good'.

Paper-cutting of all sorts keeps small children busy—under your eye of course. Plastic scissors are a useful invention for this purpose and look attractive. Try folding paper circles into segments and cutting out fascinating paper mats. Even children of four can do it. I found a small book on this subject one holiday and it helped to occupy many happy mornings. Surplus rolls of thin wall-paper can be used up, provided you press them flat first.

A mother from Ruislip describes the vivid use of scissors made by her small son. 'I found him crying because Rupert Bear, in the picture, was shut in a room and could not get out. Later he shouted, "Mummy, he can get out now, I have opened the window for him." He had cut out the little window in the picture and was waiting for Rupert to climb through.'

Do not forget to lay in a store of plasticine or other modelling material at the beginning of the holidays. Besides encouraging creative art it can be used for running repairs. Those most breakable toys—lead animals and soldiers—are all amenable to plasticine repairs, if occasionally helped with match-sticks. This kind of simple mending is quite easy and interesting for the children to do themselves.

Lastly, there are all the boxed games, waiting in shining array on the shelves of toy-shops. That leads us to the whole question of present-giving—and a new chapter.

6

Christmas—What Shall We Give Them?

Christmas is the children's festival. And, like every other birthday, this greatest of all birthdays 'comes out once a year'. So it's worth while giving some real thought to this event. We might even try, for once, to be a bit scientific about their presents.

Here, in a corner of my bedroom, is once again the familiar Mount Everest of parcels. Three weeks ago when I began collecting presents it was only a small mound. But now, so close to Christmas Day, there's a regular ice-fall of boxes. That awkward tricycle, covered over with rugs, looks like a *cwm*. Though the whole pile is hidden under a tablecloth, I know the children are as familiar as Sherpas with every angle and corner of the intriguing mountain. I only hope they haven't looked underneath . . .

Suddenly it is all over. The great Day has come and gone. The mountain has disintegrated into a vast desert of paper and string. Feeling flatter than the remains of Everest and as exhausted as its real conquerors, one instinctively hums again the familiar line. For this time its message, instead of being a spur of action, is infinitely soothing—'Christmas comes but once a year.'

But if the relief that it's over for another year is to be mingled with triumph, those parcels under the tablecloth must have been the right ones; the presents the children really wanted.

Presents, like diet, should be well-balanced and varied. So here are two things to bear in mind when you begin making your Christmas lists. First, try not to get all the same type of present. Children like presents which look, feel, and are different. Not all plastic, or all clockwork; not all the same size nor all to be used in the same mood, at the same time of year or of day, all indoors or all outdoors. With the immense variety of presents that the shops can offer today it is a mistake to do all one's buying in one department of one store.

Second, if you choose toys, make sure they are well-made and work. A toy that breaks after being used once or twice, or quickly goes wrong, is anathema. Instead of giving joy it throws the child into a state of irritation. This soon turns into rage that finally leads him into smashing up what is left of the offending present. Destruction has a sinister attraction of its own, and it is dangerous to introduce a child to its black magic by presenting him with defective toys.

Now here is a mixed diet of presents, all rich in Christmas calories.

INSTRUCTIONAL AND ARTISTIC PRESENTS—For the engineer there is Meccano with all its modern varieties, including machine tools. Building bricks in every material from wood to solid rubber are available for the young architect. If it is to be painting, experiment with some new materials—powder paints, poster paints and oils. Many teenagers who have grown tired of the box of water-colours take to oils as ducks to water. You can get brushes, a few good basic colours and boards (not expensive canvasses) for a pound or two. Oil painting gives an outlet for the teenager's creative urge. It is some-how more earthy, less unsubstantial than water-colour painting, and admirably suits their particular stage of development. It is surpris-ingly easy to make some sort of show with oils, even for children who are not supposed to be at all 'artistic'. Modelling clay has the same kind of valuable qualities, and can be bought in forms to suit every age and purse.

Cut-outs have almost every virtue for small children. They are cheap, educational and imaginatively satisfying. They look beautiful in their book or box before they are cut out, and even more beauti-ful afterwards. The hold that these miniature scenes take on a child's imagination is shown by this story from a parent in Carnforth, Lancs. She describes how her five-year-old daughter proudly showed her Coronation cut-out of Westminster Abbey to her two-year-old brother. Immediately it became the setting, in his imagination, for a *Peter Rabbit* story. 'He peered into the tiny doorway. "Where's Mr Rabbit?" he exclaimed. And he is still looking through that little doorway—for Mr Rabbit!'

GAMES FOR TWO OR MORE PLAYERS—These are a special boon during the holiday weeks. You need at least one on your list. They are socially valuable, too. For they teach children to play and get on together. In choosing boxed games, always ask how long they take to play. You need fairly short games, like card-games or race-games, for the period immediately before bedtime. It may have a fatal effect on your timetable if you have to let the children start a game like *Monopoly* half an hour before they ought to be going to bed. There are endless short race-games to choose from. Some are enchanting peeps into fairyland, others the now familiar adventure into the equally imaginary land of the rocket-ship.

Really long games, however, are most useful for filling up a whole morning. Games like *Monopoly* and *Tritactics* (a modern and more complex version of the old favourite *L'Attaque*) take literally hours to play. *Key-word*, *Scrabble* and other educational crossword games of this type take about three-quarters of an hour.

I had two childhood favourites. One was called *Princes' Quest*, the best children's race-game, played with dice, I have ever seen. But alas, it has disappeared from circulation. Little did I expect, when my uncles and aunts gave it to me for Christmas forty years ago, that my own children would be using the same enchanted board 'forty years on'. Nor did I expect that the only other family I should discover who had also played it as children would turn out to be my husband's! It was nice to have *Prince's Quest*, among other things, in common.

The other favourite was called, in those days, *Spilikins*. It was an elegant game for a steady hand, played with slender ivory sticks, exquisitely carved. This game has reappeared under curious titles, one being *Pick-a-Stick*.

COMMUNAL OR SHARED PRESENTS teach co-operation. Every family should have at least one present that belongs to all and is enjoyed by each. These shared presents help to reduce the dangers of jealousy over individual toys. Granny can often be the perfect giver for this type of present. Suggest a sledge, table-tennis or bagatelle; a wig-wam or gardening tools.

BOOKS VERSUS WHAT SOME CHILDREN CALL REAL PRESENTS— Occasionally we find a child who, though fond of reading refuses to admit that books are proper, exciting presents. The familiar oblong shape of the parcel with a book inside fails to provoke the same intrigued interest as the parcel with bulky or otherwise mysterious outlines. Children seem to prefer presents whose shapes they cannot recognise from the outside. But despite this slight handicap from which books may suffer, every child should have some books at Christmas. You can encourage them to build up a library of their own by giving a painted bookrest or shelf.

RISKY PRESENTS—Here I am not referring to explosives—air-guns or fireworks—but to certain harmless toys which are risky to choose unless you know the particular child's tastes. For some children these toys are the 'tops', for others the 'end'. Dolls and jig-saw puzzles are examples. Ninety per cent of girls love dolls at least for some periods of their childhood. But the other ten per cent feel murderous. All my four girls have asked for dolls at Christmas and birthdays. But I knew a child who always handed over a doll, if she unfortunately received one, to her brother—for decapitation. We children used to watch goggle-eyed as the heads were ranged on the park railings, to us like Tower Hill. The maternal instinct, even in girls who love dolls, is somewhat filial. It is quite normal to have 'doll crazes' lasting for several years, or perhaps only for a month or two. In between the periods of infatuation the dolls may be hurled away into a box or cupboard with the greatest callousness. I can remember treating my dolls with almost intentional savagery when they were not in favour. The 'craze' however, may go on recurring for a considerable number of years. Antonia suddenly developed her last doll phase at the age of twelve.

Here, on the other hand, is the story of a girl who never had any use for dolls at all.

'When I was a small child, every birthday and Christmas I was presented with a doll. I hated dolls, but being well brought up I thanked my parents politely, put my unwanted present with the others, and went off to play with my beloved dogs. They existed purely in my imagination. But I can still see them; Rover the collie, Gyp a nondescript brown fellow, and Spot the wire-haired terrier. By some means my wise old governess discovered my secret, and on my seventh birthday, instead of a despised doll I was greeted by a wriggling brown puppy—a real one at last!'

Relations who ask for a list of what their nieces and nephews or grandchildren would like, are great benefactors. Then if necessary one can underline *not a doll* or puzzle or card-game, whichever happens to be out of favour at the moment.

Talking of puppies, do not forget the special appeal of LIVING THINGS as presents. It may be a tiny Japanese garden, a cold-water tropical fish or a golden hamster. We have a four-year-old garden that has grown luxuriantly out of its pot, and a 'Japanese Shubunkin' (goldfish) that has lived five years in its twelve-inch tank, with the minimum of attention. But mind you make your child look after these living things herself—however much or however little care they need.

EXPENSIVE OR COMPLICATED TOYS THAT NEED SUPERVISION—If you yourself have very little time to spare or do not like playing with toys; and if your husband is not one of those useful play-addicts either, I hesitate to recommend this type of toy, at any rate for small children. Things like toy sewing-machines are wonderful, but you'll always have to be ready to help work them. Every child's mouth waters for one, but they are temperamental beauties, and seldom trouble-free in my experience. Certain types of toy cooking-stoves come into this same class. If you choose one, try to find an illustrated child's cookery book to give with it. It is a good thing to connect up your children's hobbies with reading and the world of books as early as possible.

OUTDOOR PRESENTS bring a breath of fresh air into these indoor holidays. Choose a football, bow-and-arrows, stilts, ice- or roller-skates.

If you decide on the last be generous enough to give the slightly more expensive kind of roller-skates with rubber wheels. You will earn the gratitude of many elderly people living in what they hoped were quiet squares and cul-de-sacs. They are driven mad by the screech of steel wheels on stone pavements.

USEFUL PRESENTS—The list is of course almost endless. There are all kinds of pens and pencils, particularly the handsome screw-pencil with four interchangeable colours. There is the invaluable pen- or pocket-knife. But you need to know your child before you decide on a sharp knife. It was three years before Patrick was finally able to keep his first knife permanently. He had a passion for immediately shaving off the edges of tables, so that his knife was confiscated almost as soon as it was presented. It reappeared the next birthday or Christmas, only to meet with the same fate again. Other useful presents that my daughters have continually asked for and liked are scissors, a watch, zip-up writing-case, attaché-case, plastic handbag and cabinet of drawers. The cabinet sounds rather an expensive present, but in fact you can get one under a foot high, in millboard, quite cheaply.

Most children love to have plenty of receptacles for their treasures and possessions. They are like squirrels in this respect—bent on secreting things in odd holes and corners. Every mother has noticed that if a small child finds a hole, either indoors or outdoors, his instinct is to put something into it.

Imaginative children like to endow every little niche or cavity with a mysterious use, or even inhabitant, of its own. One small girl found a piece of wall-paper torn off from her nursery wall, and some loose plaster under it. She quickly seized the opportunity to make the cavity larger. When she had scraped out a nice little hole her mother discovered it and protested, 'But Pixie Ann did it. That's where she keeps her face-powder,' explained her daughter.

When Thomas was two, and we went out for a walk, he used to point out each hole and crack in the ground and ask, 'Who lives down there?' He frequently talked of going down rabbit-holes long before I had read *Alice in Wonderland* to him. On one occasion, while reading *Peter Rabbit*, he asked, 'Why did Mr McGregor catch Peter Rabbit's father, when he must have been able to run much faster than Peter?' Then he added, 'We'll have to squeeze down a rabbit-hole and find out from the rabbits' dictionary.'

I have never found any form of bag or box to fail as a present. Children like collecting things in small spaces, just as they enjoy creeping into small spaces themselves. No doubt the fact that they were so comfortable in a small space, before birth, has something to do with it. But psychology apart, 'a case of one's own' always makes a useful present.

HOME-MADE VERSUS SHOP PRESENTS—A toy made by father, or set of doll's clothes made by mother, is a special thrill. So are hand-painted presents and home-made woolly toys. But don't let your craftsman's pride tempt you into supplying all the presents. The high gloss and professionally finished appearance of a shop toy has some-thing attractive of its own, and something which the child will miss, if everything is home-made. Here is a four-year-old child's reaction to a toy that conspicuously lacked that finished appearance. 'My friend borrowed my paint-sprayer to paint his car, on condition that he sprayed Peter's tricycle at the same time. Pressed for time, he gave the tricycle a very quick coat. The following day I was up a ladder painting the gutter when Peter cycled past muttering, "I call this bitty painting … bitty painting." "Bitty painting?" I asked, puzzled. He pointed to his tricycle; "Well, this is a bitty painted and this is a bitty didn't!"' Children do not like 'bitty' presents.

It is also sometimes difficult to keep home-made toys a com-plete surprise—one of the essential elements in a successful present. However, this is by no means an insuperable difficulty. Children are easily hood-winked, and grown-ups can be very ingenious. I remember my nurse making me a white robe one Christmas for my baby doll. She made it all the while I was in the nursery, and to my perpetual inquiries as to what she was doing, she replied that it was a dress for my baby brother. When I protested that the sleeves were much too small to fit his arms, she explained that they were not sleeves, but a new-fashioned kind of trimming, designed to hang over each shoulder. When the robe was finally presented to me, though I did indeed recognise it, it somehow looked quite different from the curious garment I had watched in the making.

But if you over-do the home-made presents, even with the best intentions, you may get a rebuff like this mother from Wallasey, Cheshire. 'I made my four-year-old daughter a red velvet hat from some left-over material. She looked at the hat, then said, "Is that for me?" "Yes," I replied. "Well, I would rather have a *buyed* hat."'

I must end with what I can only describe as Just Toys—humming-tops, jack-in-the-boxes, wire-haired stair hounds. They are not educational, occupational or any other long word. But they are *fun*—as all good toys should be.

7

Leading Your Child to a Good Book

As we saw in the last chapter, books are not always the most popular presents. Need this be? In this chapter I want to strike a blow for good books. Today a three-cornered battle rages between books, comics and TV. Sometimes the rivals are all-against-all; sometimes there are alliances, as when 'Andy Pandy' finds his way into *Robin*, or a TV version of *Westward Ho!* and *The Secret Garden* whets the children's appetites for books.

People often think that comics spoil the children's taste for really good reading matter. There is a fatalistic feeling abroad that soon only grammar school boys will read books at all. The comic-bred child will pass into the modern secondary school, where he will be taught not by book, but by the TV screen.

Personally I believe these three antagonists should be allies in the cause of education. The role of TV in this triumvirate is too complex to be discussed here. But the two 'reading partners' can be brought face to face. First I want to suggest that comics are not necessarily the enemies of good books. Second, that there is a way of making good books far more acceptable to children than they often are.

A correspondent from Bristol describes what great readers her family of ten were, and adds, 'We read everything that came our way, from Dickens to *Comic Cuts*.' I wonder if other parents would agree with me that these children were right to read everything—including comics? Or do some of them never let comics darken their doors? Here is an argument between an ardent comic-hater and a mother who witnesses an influx of comics every week and does not mind. In the course of this set-to you will see many of the points for and against comics brought out.

Should We Ban the Comics?

Comic-hater: Surely, Mrs X, you would not deny that the subject-matter of comics has always been contemptible? Nowadays, under Transatlantic influences, comics are brutal, violent, sexy, illiterate and slang-crammed. They have become moral sinks and literary rubbish dumps. They are …

Mother (emerging from behind *Eagle* to face the storm): I'm afraid you are banning all comics because some—mostly not published in Britain—admittedly offend. Of course there are comics and comics. I will agree that we parents should keep a sharp look-out on the type of comics our *teenagers* buy. That's where bad influences—sex and sadism—are most likely to creep in. Incidentally, I do not think it is a good thing for mothers to leave too many women's maga-zines lying about the house, when they have a young teenager at home. Sentimental lovestories, though harmless in themselves, seize the imagination of young girls and 'put ideas into their heads' which are incompatible with ordinary school life. They begin to fall in love with love, if not with a person, and become restless and dissatisfied. Nature has made it hard enough for them as it is to cope with their new physical instincts. We should not make it even harder by allow-ing them to feed on literature appropriate to girls in their twenties. We must give them literature and art which will help them to sub-limate their sex-instincts for the next five or six years; the poems of Keats, or creative work with needle, clay or paint.

But whereas teenagers may easily be in danger from too many magazines or certain kinds of comics, the younger children can devour comics and suffer no ill effects. Let us look at the contents of a typical comic. Detective-stories, thrillers …

Comic-hater: There, what did I say? Thrillers? Trash! Fixing the chil-dren's minds on fantastic nonsense like space-men and moon-rockets when they ought to be learning about the real world. No wonder young people can't settle down these days, with all that trash in their heads!

Mother: On the contrary, the child's instinct for adventure is a priceless gift. Without it, no one would grow up to be an inventor or explorer. We should have no knowledge of the air above us or the sea around us. Today their imaginations go to the moon. Tomorrow their bodies may follow. You used to read Jules Verne. Why shouldn't they read Dan Dare?

Comic-hater: There you go again! Fancy comparing the works of a classical author like Jules Verne with a character from a comic serial! The language of comics is nothing but slang, interspersed with horrible animal noises—'sproing', 'eek', 'whee-ee-ee', 'womp', 'gocher'.

Mother: That's the vernacular of today. I agree it isn't pretty. Nor is the sound of a motor-cycle roaring down the street. You must expect a noisy age to speak sometimes in noisy, undignified accents.

But you exaggerate the amount of 'trash' in comics. Have you ever read a typical comic right through? It is full of variety—history, nature-study, domestic hints (my daughters learned how to make a bed properly last week—from a comic. They took it from a comic where they would not listen to me!), puzzles, topical information, Bible stories, and stories of the saints. I once found the best account of David and Jonathan I have ever read, outside the Old Testament, in a comic.

Comic-hater: What about the small type these stories are printed in? It ruins their eyesight.

Mother: Nonsense. An old wives' tale! If the light is good and the child's eyes are normal, he can focus small print and large, just as legs can run fast or slow.

Rationing Comics

These are some of the main arguments advanced for and against comics. Personally, I take an intermediate line between these two positions. There is no need to make a tragedy of comics. Let the children read. Let them acquire a real taste for it. Even if they will only read *Robin* now, it may well encourage them to read *A Midsummer Night's Dream* later. The essential thing is that they should learn to read and love reading.

But the reading of comics can be carried to excess.

Personally, I should neither ban comics altogether, nor allow them to be consumed in unlimited quantities. I agree with the wife of a London lorry driver, herself a reader of poetry and literature, who has this to say on comics. 'Comics are so easy to read that what we call "good books" will be left unopened unless the comics are wisely rationed.'

In our household I try to see that only a limited number of comics is bought each week. We have three comics among our five younger children. Of course children also swop comics at school, thus increasing the weekly comic ration. On the other hand, the amount of time they spend on each comic is remarkably small. My children are done with a copy in twenty minutes at the most, and ready for some more sustaining literature.

Another mother, who had been very strictly chaperoned in her own reading during childhood, so that she secretly devoured all kinds of unsuitable books with very little understanding of their spicy contents—this parent decided her children must be given complete freedom of the printed word.

'There have been times,' she writes, 'when we have shuddered at comics or thrillers of dubious reputation; but the book has either been put down as not much "cop" or else read and very little absorbed of doubtful value. A child's mind obviously absorbs only that which really interests it, and that is not often harmful. It is our adult knowledge of the world which makes us parents fear for our children's minds.'

'To the pure all things are pure' is a good motto for parents inclined towards over-censorship. But it is possible for pure minds to be corrupted, poisoned by bad books, unless they are provided with the antidote. *A love for good books* is the best antidote. But the rationing of comics and thrillers does not in itself develop a taste for good literature. How are we parents to inculcate this taste, so that the negative method of rationing inferior books may be supplemented and strengthened by a positive love for the classics?

Fortunately there is an altogether simple and delightful method of leading children to good books available to every parent. In my own experience this method is fool-proof. It works with even the most book-shy child. You just lead your child to the waters of literature and it drinks! This truly magical solution is, in two words, *reading aloud*.

Reading Aloud

Now at this point I can hear parents muttering indignantly: 'Teaching her grandmother to suck eggs ... Of course we read aloud to our children!' Yes, but I do not just mean reading a page or two out of the book that has been thrust under your nose more and more insistently during the last ten minutes, with a shriller and shriller appeal: 'Mummy, read to me, *read to me*, READ TO ME!'

No, I mean something far more systematic and serious. If reading aloud is to achieve its finest possible results it must be developed into a science, an art, an education.

And first, what are these fine results? To begin with, reading a 'good book' aloud transforms it, as if with a magic wand, from a slow-moving, difficult task, into an absorbing and exciting story. This applies particularly to children's classics. We parents are too apt to push a famous classic, say Charles Kingsley's *The Water Babies*, into our children's hands and then grumble when they refuse to read it. How many mothers and fathers have actually read it themselves since their nursery days, and remember what it is like? Do they realise that this wonderful children's classic, suffused with imagination and throbbing with drama is also stuffed with pages and pages of abstruse argumentation? Here is a typical passage from the last chapter (there are many worse ones than this!):

> Then Tom came to the island of Polupragmosyne ... and a very noisy place it is, as might be expected, considering that all the inhabitants are ex-officio on the wrong side of the house in the Parliament of Man, and the Federation of the World ...

I have just finished reading *The Water Babies* aloud to Kevin and Catherine. The fascination of the story gripped them as no comic ever has. But for me it was an arduous task. Words needed explaining on every page. Long passages had to be skipped entirely. (Incidentally, it is surprising how expert one soon becomes at glancing ahead and skipping an unsuitable passage, without the slightest hitch or hesitation in the course of reading.) But it is just because reading aloud is an art, requiring practice and persistence, that it is so worth while. In reading to your child, you take on yourself some of the difficulties that might have kept him from the classics.

You need not always read the whole of a 'good book' aloud. Some children like to be helped over the slow beginning. Then they will carry on by themselves. I have found this method work well with books like Sir Walter Scott's *Ivanhoe*, Dickens' *Bleak House* and Bulwer Lytton's *The Last Days of Pompeii*. All these have thrilling plots, once you can break through the portentous introductions.

Or again, a younger child may start a book on his own, and then need a leg-up at some point when the story seems to lag. It is a great mistake to drive a child on with a book he is thoroughly bored by. On the other hand, you must not allow him to form the habit of giving up in the middle. Reading some parts of the book aloud is the solution. There is no need to be inflexible or dogmatic about whether you read a certain book to your child, or whether he reads it to himself. Let him alternate between the two if that is the way in which he will enjoy the book most.

I believe reading aloud should be a real family institution. It should begin at the age of one, and continue as long as the family is together. I first showed Antonia the *Babar* books when she was ten months old. Very soon 'showing pictures' developed into 'telling the story' too. At about three years old she began to say, 'Don't *tell the story*, read it.' From four to eleven I read aloud every children's classic under the sun. The fact that she learnt to read to herself very early did not in any way cut short my periods of reading aloud. For a child, reading a book to one's self curled up in a secluded corner has delights of its own. But it in no way takes the place of the special pleasures of being read to.

The Art of Reading Aloud

Here are a few suggestions on the art of reading aloud for the parent who is not yet an adept, but intends to become one.

1 Have a regular time every day for reading aloud. I find just before bedtime the best, and after lunch also, during the holidays. Never miss your session. Reading aloud should be a family ritual. Kevin refers to it as 'my reading' and will not go to bed without it. It ranks in importance with 'my dinner' or 'my walk'. I must admit that these sessions take up a good deal of time, especially if there are several children of different ages needing separate spells of reading aloud. But once the habit is formed and the necessary time set aside it becomes a stimulating and peaceful part of family life.

Many parents have written testifying to the important place reading aloud occupies in their own families. Here is a mother of three from Surbiton, Surrey: 'Our practice was a chapter or so every night at least, after prayers, and a look at the pictures. We read every classic available; also poetry and children's plays. We each took parts. Today my children, aged 15, 12, and 10, have a better grasp of books and poetry than many adults. They enjoy radio and television classics brought to life from the baby days, and at the local school were all congratulated on their familiarity with books the average child has never heard of.' This proud parent adds ruefully that none of these avid readers can spell! But the family ritual of reading aloud has enabled them to carry all else before them.

Reading aloud should be regarded as a pleasure, not as a utilitarian matter. But most parents would agree that it has in fact helped their children very greatly in education and general culture. A mother from Liverpool, for instance, writes that her son of eleven did not seem to be 'over-intelligent' in his class, so that when he sat for the exam she had not much hope of his passing. When the results came out, however, he was the only boy in his form who passed. 'I feel sure now that my early reading aloud to him, and his own reading, must have been a bigger help to him than I realised. So now I try not to get cross when he has his head stuck in a book and doesn't hear when I speak to him. Evidently he has gleaned enough information from his reading to pass the intelligence side of the exam. I am encouraging my daughter, aged six, to read all she can for the time when her turn comes to sit for the scholarship.'

2 Always have the children really close to you while reading, the youngest on your lap, the others on each side, or even on the chair arms, so that they can see the print. Children of seven upwards love to follow the written word. It helps their own reading, and teaches them how to pronounce new words. How often has Catherine said in amazement, 'Oh, I always thought that word was pronounced like *this* …' uttering some strange mispronunciation of her own.

3 Small children need a picture on *every* page. Some children's books are misguidedly bound with two consecutive pages of solid print opposite each other, followed by two pictures facing each other. The whole point of pictures for small children who cannot yet read to themselves is that they should be able to look at the pictures while you are reading the text to them. Many otherwise brilliant picture books have this fatal flaw. The interest of a four-year-old flags if he has nothing but print to look at while you are reading to him.

4 Don't try reading long stories aloud till the children are of school age. Before five, the child likes to hear a *complete* story every time you read to him. Even Catherine, at seven, could hardly bear to wait for the end of *The Water Babies*—which took us a fortnight to read. But when we got on to *King Arthur's Knights* she had become acclimatised to the chapter-by-chapter method.

5 Don't worry if your child demands to be read the same book over and over again. This does not indicate a lack of enterprise or intelligence. Children love to know their books by heart. Repetition is part of the ritual.

6 At about seven or eight a child will begin to feel competent to read aloud herself to a younger brother or sister. No need to dilate on the obvious advantages of this development! Just encourage it.

7 Reading aloud need not stop altogether even when the children are in their teens. Patrick, at thirteen, greatly enjoyed reading Shakespeare aloud with me. (Parents mustn't mind if they tend to get the less star-parts—Messengers and Attendants.) Incidentally, *all* reading aloud, not only Shakespeare's plays, should be highly

dramatic. Parents must learn to change their voices to suit the characters in the story. If you have never tried this before, read *Alice* or *The Jungle Books* for a start. It is impossible not to act the superb characters in these classics.

An author of children's books writes to me in the hope that reading aloud may yet save our children's interest in stories dealing with subjects other than Supermen and Atomic Jets. He adds, 'If the Reader-Aloud will modulate the voice to suit the characters in the story (Dickens used to do it) it will go over with a resounding bang and give the narrator much more interest in the task.' The latter is an important point.

8 I hesitate before making this last suggestion. It is about something that was done by the first Elizabethans. It continued down to our Victorian grandparents. Even Edwardians sometimes did it. Only in this age has it died out. Why not revive reading aloud by adults to each other?

I sometimes read aloud to my husband. We both enjoy it—for five minutes. Somehow my voice has a mysteriously soporific effect. Very soon I find I am reading to a 'sleeping partner'.

Which are the Classics?

It appears, from various inquiries I have received, some from as far away as Australia, that many parents are anxious to read the classics to their children, but are not sure which books are classics.

Without being dogmatic on this subject, I feel it may be helpful to end this chapter with a short list of books which I myself consider would undoubtedly make the grade. Who knows but that the increase of good reading among our children may even benefit parents too. As a librarian from Adelaide, South Australia, puts it: 'Through their children, many parents are reading books for the first time in their lives. Today children frequently come in the library with this request, "Please can I keep that book another day? Mum's reading it!"'

Classics for younger children:

Peter Rabbit Books	Beatrix Potter
Just So Stories	Kipling
Jungle Books	Kipling
Alice in Wonderland	Lewis Carroll
Through the Looking-glass	Lewis Carroll
Grimm's Fairy Tales	
Hans Andersen's Fairy Tales	
Andrew Lang's Fairy Books	
The Water Babies	Charles Kingsley
Tales of King Arthur and the Round Table	
Tales of Robin Hood	
Myths of Greece and Rome	
Norse Tales	
Aesop's Fables	
Robinson Crusoe	Daniel Defoe
Gulliver's Travels	Swift
Struwelpeter	Hoffman
The Book of Nonsense	Edward Lear
Cautionary Tales	Hilaire Belloc
The Bad Child's Book of Beasts	Hilaire Belloc
Pinocchio	Collodi
A Wonder Book and Tanglewood Tales	Nathaniel Hawthorne
Black Beauty	Anna Sewell
The Enchanted Castle	E. Nesbit
The Treasure Seekers	E. Nesbit
The Would-be-Goods	E. Nesbit

Classics for older children:
(though you cannot draw a hard and fast line about age)

Little Men	Louisa Alcott
Little Women	Louisa Alcott
Good Wives	Louisa Alcott
Jo's Boys	Louisa Alcott
The Little Duke	Charlotte Yonge
What Katy Did	Susan Coolidge

What Katy Did at School	Susan Coolidge
What Katy Did Next	Susan Coolidge
Puck of Pook's Hill	Kipling
Kim	Kipling
Treasure Island	R.L. Stevenson
Kidnapped	R.L. Stevenson
Catriona	R.L. Stevenson
The Black Arrow	R.L. Stevenson
The Master of Ballantrae	R.L. Stevenson
The Princess and the Goblins	George Macdonald
The Princess and Curdie	George Macdonald
The Wind in the Willows	Kenneth Grahame
Tom Brown's Schooldays	Hughes
The Last Days of Pompeii	Bulwer Lytton
The Woman in White	Wilkie Collins
The Moonstone	Wilkie Collins
Children of the New Forest	Captain Marryat
Sherlock Holmes	Conan Doyle
The Tower of London	Harrison Ainsworth
Old Saint Paul's	Harrison Ainsworth
Windsor Castle	Harrison Ainsworth
Vanity Fair	Thackeray
Henry Esmond	Thackeray
Ivanhoe	Sir Walter Scott
The Talisman	Sir Walter Scott
The Tale of Two Cities	Charles Dickens
Oliver Twist	Charles Dickens
Great Expectations	Charles Dickens
David Copperfield	Charles Dickens
Bleak House	Charles Dickens
Pickwick Papers	Charles Dickens
Nicholas Nickleby	Charles Dickens
Emma	Jane Austen
Pride and Prejudice	Jane Austen
Jane Eyre	Charlotte Bronte
Wuthering Heights	Emily Bronte

8

Father Christmas—To Be or Not To Be?

Every year, as the children's great festival comes round again, someone takes a pot-shot at Father Christmas. Sometimes they shoot to kill. He's a rogue, a swindler, a betrayer of the children's trust, a relic of past superstitions unworthy of this scientific age. More often they only shoot at the excrescences that have grown up on the surface of this genial giant. They attack the commercialism that defaces him. He's become just another sales-pusher, they say, paraded around the streets and shops while December 25th is still out of sight and hearing.

But even if this is true and I agree in deploring the commercialism that so often reduces the Christmas saint to a rather pitiable old man—why throw away the baby with the bath water? Father Christmas is a gala event in the child's fantasy life. Belief in him has its roots in deep human needs. Myth, legend and truth are all inextricably woven around his person. So parents, give him a reprieve and welcome him into your homes again this year!

Why do I say that Father Christmas is necessary to the child? It could be proved by delving into psychology or theology. But let us not go beyond the observation of every parent. What do we notice about our children's relations with Father Christmas? That *they*, not we create him. Parents may launch the idea of Santa Claus. It is the children themselves who keep him afloat, pilot him through rough seas of scepticism, contradiction, denial. Refuse to have him drowned even when all the facts are against him.

You must have noticed the reluctance of children to stop believing in him. They suspect or are told that 'It's only Daddy', but they still cling to shreds of the legend. 'I know it's a man who comes with the sack of toys after tea,' said Catherine at seven, 'but it's the *real* Father Christmas who fills our stockings in the night, isn't it?' Even Judith, when she was ten years old and had long ceased to believe either in the 'day' or 'night' Father Christmas, confessed to feeling a thrill of inexplicable excitement when she hung up her stocking and turned off the light on Christmas Eve. There was going to be a midnight visitor . . .

Children, in their efforts to save their mysterious friend from destruction, are ingenious at adapting him to modern conditions. A mother from Wirral, Cheshire, writes to say that she is forced by her son to leave a key in the front door on Christmas Eve because he objects to the narrowness of the chimney. Father Christmas then descends by plane with a co-pilot called Bill. Supper is left for them as they will be cold and hungry after their long journey. The small boy follows the journey from Lapland to Cheshire on a map, and does a rapid bunk upstairs to bed when he calculates they are about to land.

A Birmingham mother describes how her daughter completely identified herself with the legend and ingeniously made her way into the picture. 'She used to pretend she was the favourite doll of Santa Claus, and accompanied him on all his exciting journeys. I would sometimes get cross when she careered about yelling her orders to the reindeer.'

Children will often deliberately rope in facts to build up their beloved fantasy, instead of using facts, as grown-ups do, to destroy it. They feel the need of proofs and evidence—and behold! the proofs are there, right under their noses, in the every day world around them. A Walsall, Staffs., father was shown the tracks of the milk-cart in the snow which had fallen on Christmas Eve. 'Look Daddy,' exclaimed his son, 'you can see where Santa Claus has been in his sled to all the childrens houses.'

The mother of twins in Middlesex tried to give a scientific explanation of a natural phenomenon, but her twins preferred a

Christmas interpretation of their own. 'My four-year-old twins were out walking on a late afternoon shortly after Christmas and we saw a particularly beautiful sunset. James asked, "What are all those pretty red lines in the sky?" I tried to give the practical explanation of the reflection of the sun's rays upon the clouds. Michael, however, strongly disagreed, saying that they were God's decorations for his Christmas tree. "Oh, yes," added James, "and when it's dark. He switches on the lovely lights."'

If we attempt to trace the popularity of the Father Christmas fantasy with children, we find that it follows the line of their own imaginative development. As their fantasy life grows, the myth grows too; when this period begins to pass, the myth fades. Before children are two years old they 'see through' things in a way that slightly older children are unable to do. This is because their imaginative life is not yet strong enough to blind them to reality. Between two and three the fantasy life develops, obscuring 'reality'. It continues in full vigour until five or six. Then diminishes. It is precisely during these years—three to six—that Father Christmas reigns in their hearts.

Antonia was first visited by Father Christmas when she was just two. She behaved perfectly politely towards him, showing neither fear nor excitement. But while she was having her bath that evening and talk turned on the presents Father Christmas had brought, she remarked to me quite casually, 'Father Christmas was Dada ...' She had seen through it. But a year later this realistic approach had vanished! Even the memory of it disappeared. From three to seven Antonia was a lyrical believer, talking about him with awe and intense fervour.

Parents who enter into the Christmas game with a will may be in for a few surprises. For the child's imagination will stop at nothing. A Sussex mother, for instance, sends this account of a Christmas disaster: 'When my boy was just three years old a friend put her hand up her bedroom chimney and produced a choc bar saying "Father Christmas must have put it there!" A few days later I saw a black object descending our stairs. "I put my head up my bedroom chimney," he explained, "to see if Father Christmas had left me another choc bar, and all the soot fell on me!"'

If they are Scared …

Fear is never far removed from the fantasy life of small children, and it frequently intrudes to mar the joys of Father Christmas's visits, unless the parents take trouble in advance to prevent it doing so. Toddlers are often scared of the tall figure in the scarlet robe with a strangely deep voice and flowing white beard. So always pick them up when you hear him coming, just in case. And keep on the outside of the circle. Maybe your baby will be lion-hearted and demand to go nearer. But wait till he does so!

If you have a nervous older child in your family—too old to be picked up but not old enough to face the awe-inspiring figure calmly—try this solution. Hatch out a comic act with your Santa Claus. Father will then emphasise the jovial, rather than the mysterious side of Santa Claus's character. One Christmas Day my husband hobbled in announcing that poor Father Christmas had got rheumatism in the Arctic. The children, even the timid ones, shrieked with joy. When he accidentally slipped on the lino and toppled over, their cup was full. In the general scrimmage that followed no one noticed the yards of familiar trousers showing under the scarlet robe.

Some children are fearful of the Christmas Eve visit. Particularly they fear lest they will not fall asleep in time, and Father Christmas, when he finds them still awake, will pass them by. Most children can be easily reassured on this point. 'Father Christmas is magic. However late you get to sleep he will never miss you out. So don't worry.' But if this does not work and the over-excited child gets real insomnia, let her hang her stocking in another room. Try the hall or the kitchen, as they do on the Continent. Incidentally, I always put on the full regalia to fill the stockings—a lengthy proceeding—in case some light sleeper wakes. But no one ever has.

From Myth to Reality

What about the *transition* from belief in Santa Claus to disbelief? 'A boy told me at school. . . . There's no such thing as Father Christmas.'

Must your child make such a crushingly bleak transition as this? To say there is no such thing as Father Christmas is to carry fact to the point of pure materialism. Because this very thing so often happens I know of one sincere and thoughtful parent who refused to allow his children *ever* to believe in the Christmas myth. He feared that when disillusionment came they would reject the whole Christmas Story, truth as well as fairy-tale. He imagined them saying to themselves 'Well, if Santa Claus is not true, what about God? . . .'

I do not think that this difficulty is as serious as perhaps it seems. A perfectly natural transition exists in the person of Santa Claus himself. Why not tell the children who Santa Claus really was? The children's saint, Saint Nikolaus (Santa Klaus) from Bohemia. This is the time, too, to recall to them the true Christmas story. Then they need not stop believing that *someone else*, besides Daddy and Mummy and Aunt Mary, sends them good things at Christmas.

9

Christmas Day Without Tears

A mother from Hemel Hempstead sent me a problem which she felt would be troubling countless young parents on Christmas Day. 'My four-year-old girl is a normally well-behaved child. But at Christmas all the excitement and numerous presents (only one big one from us, the rest from relations) make her lose her good manners, and she seems bored even with her new toys. Our last three Christmases have had tears—such a pity after all the weeks we spend preparing and looking forward to it.'

How many parents can boast that this minor tragedy has never happened in their family? Few, I suspect. I myself remember one such occasion. It was 5.30 p.m. on Christmas Day, near the end of the day for a three-year-old. My youngest sat on the floor surrounded by a derelict area of torn paper and empty boxes. Toys lay among the debris like furniture after a bomb has fallen. Every time Father Christmas brought out a present from his sack there was a plaintive cry, 'me! me!' Each time the parcel went to another member of the family, an angry wail arose, 'More … more …' He refused to play with the toys he had already got. When bedtime finally came he left in a mood from which 'comfort and joy' were conspicuously silent.

I learnt several things from this unhappy experience. Two mistakes are generally responsible for those Christmas tears. Mothers save up the most dramatic event of the festival—Father Christmas's visit—until *too late* in the day, when the younger children are already beginning to get tired. And they allow *too many* presents to appear all at once.

Too many and too late. King John died of a surfeit of lampreys. A child's joy in Christmas can die of a surfeit of presents.

I find it best to invite Father Christmas well before tea-time when there are toddlers in the family. This gives them a chance to 'go off the boil' before bedtime.

In our family, present-giving has a strict time-table. Thus it is spread evenly over the day, like this; *Crack of dawn*: Opening stockings. *Breakfast*: Children pile plates with presents to each other and to parents. *After Breakfast*: Parents give one big present to each child. *Afternoon*: Father Christmas brings presents from relations, Godparents, friends. Children should give as well as receive. Boys and girls like doing things themselves, even better than having lovely things done for them. That's the snag of Christmas Day. The children are apt to become passive receivers of our bounty. And this role eventually cloys.

The solution is simple. It begins before the great day. Encourage your child to buy, make, wrap and send as many presents as possible himself. Let him have a festival of giving on Christmas Day.

In the letter quoted at the beginning of this chapter, the mother who wrote it included the following question: 'Will the new baby make a difference this time?' In my reply to her I suggested that the new arrival should indeed help in solving the problem. 'It might be an idea to appear to consult your daughter about Baby's Christmas presents, and to discuss how to give Baby a happy time without upsetting the routine by too much excitement and noise. In this way you may indirectly get her own reactions to the great day; and at the same time help her by making her think about giving others pleasure, as well as getting a lot herself. You could also encourage her to plan surprises for her father—and she will be sure to spend secret energy on planning for you too.'

Children's presents to their parents must, of course, be a surprise. Surprises they often are. 'My little boy of three,' writes a Newport mother, 'gave me some dirty-looking flowers, saying: "There are some flowers to wear in your hair." As I was arranging them in my hair I asked him where he got them. He promptly answered, "Out of the dust-bin, Mummy".'

It is a good thing for children who get a great many presents to give away toys to those who get very few. Occasionally, however, small children offer broken toys. 'This dolly's lost her leg. I'll give her away.' Discourage this, although you should not insist on their giving away a favourite.

Presents from children to each other seem to have a special effect. They inspire more genuine gratitude than do presents from grown-ups, which are too often taken for granted. But a child readily appreciates the sacrifice another child has made. Here is an Essex mother's story of an Easter present. 'Having saved her pocket-money, Vivien, aged seven, bought an Easter egg for Mummy and Daddy. Then she turned to her sister, aged five, and said with a wave of her hand to the counter, "Now what would you like, Christine?" Christine selected a chocolate bar, and evidently much impressed by this generosity, turned to Vivien on leaving the shop and said, "You know, you are so good and kind people ought to call you *Saint Vivien!*"'

On December 30th I received a second letter from Hemel Hempstead. 'It is with pleasure that I write to tell you that this Christmas there were no tears. Our four-year-old daughter had immense fun wrapping up parcels for other people. But for the first time she managed to undo the strings of her parcels on Christmas morning unaided, so that I don't know which present came from whom. No doubt by next year we shall have found the answer to that one!'

I too have found it a problem to keep track of the presents, especially when a large family are sitting round all opening them as fast as they can at once. I am afraid that a certain amount of discipline has had to be introduced into our present-opening ceremony, now that the number of children has out-stripped the number of grown-ups able to supervise them. The children who are able to write are each given a piece of paper and pencil and admonished without fail to write down the name of the giver and the gift immediately a parcel is opened. Those who cannot write are allowed an older brother or sister as amanuensis. Proceedings are still rather hectic, but at least I do not have to send off a string of thank-you letters all simply naming in the vaguest terms, 'your lovely present'. But occasionally, even now, there is a slip-up. How one blesses the incredibly efficient and kind donor who puts the gifts name as well as her own on the label inside!

Moderation in All Things

Too much and too rich—that is another problem. It applies to food, of course. Few small children can cope with all the traditional Christmas fare. But they make valiant efforts. The plum pudding challenges them because of its buried treasure. As for that Christmas cake … The 'white peril' it becomes after Christmas is nothing to its menace on the day. My advice is—give it a miss. Jellies and fruit are more acceptable for tea, after all that has gone before.

Apart from present-giving and receiving, children need activity on Christmas Day. Let them sing carols while waiting for Father Christmas to arrive, or after he has departed. These things break the monotony of presents, the feeling that it is almost a duty to play with the new toys all the time.

It is important to stick to your child's routine to a certain extent even on Christmas Day. Young Children are creatures of habit. Too great a departure from normality upsets them. So try not to abandon the main features of your child's day even on this special occasion. Take her for the usual walk. Perhaps to deliver presents to her friends. Perhaps to visit some lonely old person. Put her to bed a little earlier than usual rather than letting her stay up later 'for a treat'. Many children have been awake since 4 or 5 a.m., for somehow the bulging stocking seems to act like a very early alarm clock. I remember one fatal Christmas when the older children, on returning from the midnight service, accidentally woke up the little ones. There was a great opening of small parcels in stockings at two o'clock in the morning—and many yawns the next day.

I always wind up Christmas Day with a spell of quiet reading aloud. Sometimes, if the children seem over-excited, I find it better to choose an old favourite from among the books instead of a new

Christmas one. The old one is not so stimulating as the new and introduces a peaceful feeling of familiarity before sleep time.

Everyone is tired at the end of it all, parents and children alike. But how wonderful it is when the tiredness is an expression of fulfilment rather than satiety. Then there are no tears, but heart-felt thanks; such as one mother was fortunate enough to overhear, as she passed her daughter's open door: '... and thank you, God, for a lovely day. I enjoyed it, and I hope you did too.'

10

'I'm Giving a Party ...'

Someone once said: 'Everyone is either a born host or a born guest.' Luckily children are born both. If anything, they incline slightly to the role of host. Going to a party is bliss—giving one is ecstasy. So if your child says wistfully, 'I do wish I could have a party before school begins again ...' forget that Christmas is only just over, and go ahead. Do you hesitate because of the expense and trouble involved? There is no need to be daunted. The best parties are not always the ultra lavish ones. Indeed, the secret of a successful party is to let your child do everything possible herself.

If she is old enough to want to give a party she is old enough to do most of the organising for it. A mother from Barnsley, Yorkshire, describes how her eleven-year-old son, Kevin, organised his own Coronation Party. 'The children up our way discovered they were the only ones not having a Coronation Party. So they decided to do it themselves. Committee was formed, money-box appeared, list of subscriptions made, raffle tickets sold, tea begged. Result, a wonderful party, including presents for each child, ice-cream, the Queen's health drunk in lemonade, fireworks. Weren't we parents proud?'

Beginning with the invitations, you need not buy printed ones. Your child will enjoy making them. All you need do is to provide one model. Otherwise something vital is likely to be left out; the date or time or address.

Now the tea. The proof of the party is in the eating. Somehow tea is the central fact of the party, like the transformation scene at the pantomime. It may not be your favourite item, but it is the touchstone. If that fails, all fails.

Here again, a girl of ten or eleven can help a lot. Perhaps she has already learnt how to make biscuits and small cakes. If not, now's the time to let her start. She can certainly make the sandwiches. And we all know egg sandwiches are party priorities. This is the age of savouries. Children prefer salt. They reject too many sugary cakes. A story from Paignton illustrates the need to cater carefully for the tastes of our sophisticated children: 'My small niece Julie, aged three-and-a-half, likes savouries and at the party she could see nothing in that line. Her hostess tried again and again to tempt her, only to be met with a firm headshake. Suddenly, to everyone's embarrassment, Julie blurted out, "I'd rather have a sausage!"' For drinks, you need not bother to get in extra milk. Milk or tea is not regarded as party fare. A packet of straws and some bottles of squash or pop are what you need.

Then the place arrangement. Your child can do it all. Let her make a list of guests first. Then name-cards for each place. She can decorate these like the invitation cards, giving a kind of visual 'signature tune' to her party. Catherine, whose second name is Rose, had a fine time making invitation and name-cards for her birthday party. She adorned them all with symbolic roses, and spent many happy hours thus 'gainfully employed'.

Whatever you do, don't leave small children to choose their own places. If you do, there is likely to be an ugly rush to sit by the 'birthday girl' or hostess, and an even uglier rush to avoid certain other fellow-guests—often the one or two boys who slip into a girls' party. Also, in a large party one is apt to lay the wrong number of plates unless they are firmly labelled. If your daughter insists, as is often the case, on asking the whole of her class to her party, it is possible to dispense with chair and name-cards altogether, and let them stand up for tea at a buffet table. It is not suitable for smaller children, but my school-age children prefer it because it is unusual and therefore more of a treat.

At a sit-down tea, two other things make the whole difference to the table. Crackers and candles. Miniature crackers are an intriguing change and very cheap. But be warned! Do not allow some enthusiastic boy to start the cracker-pulling before tea is begun. If you do, it will be a shambles. No food will be eaten, so that tea will not last the scheduled half-hour. And your pretty table will look a wreck before anyone has had time to take it in and admire the decor. The only exceptions I occasionally make to this rule are parties for the three and four-year-olds. Sometimes, at this stage, party manners are too good; silence reigns, and an early burst of cracker-fire is needed to break the ice.

You must not be disappointed and think your party a flop if some of the children seem to eat little. Excitement often kills appetite. It is no good pressing them. If you do, their plates will just pile up with uneaten dainties—one bite out of each. Young Jack was suffering from an over-hospitable hostess. She asked him several times to have some more. After repeating No four times, when asked again he said in a loud voice, 'No! When I say No I mean NOT!' Another child, who had appeared to have made a hearty meal and enjoyed the feast thoroughly, was congratulated by her pleased hostess on her nice clean plate. The child's adult next-door neighbour tactfully did not reveal that everything had been quietly, and with no word spoken, slipped on to her plate.

Party Games

Now for the games. The best ice-breaker is Musical Bumps. If you have no piano or gramophone, just clap your hands. It works quite as well. Make the bigger children dance with their backs towards you. If you want a game to break the sound barrier, my choice is Dressing-up Relay Race. Two teams are lined up side by side. The leading child races forward to a heap of clothes (big gloves, coat, trousers, cap, etc.), dresses up, runs round his line, undresses, and runs back to the end of the line. Next child repeats till one team wins. Prizes can be a sweet each.

The Balloon Game is another excellent, noisy team game. The opposing teams sit facing each other, toe to toe (in order to keep the lines straight) and the umpire drops a balloon into the lines, like a football into a scrum. Both sides bat the balloon wildly to and fro, and whenever it touches the floor or hits the wall behind one of the teams, the other team scores a goal.

A third team game of a more decorous type is King's Jelly. This is a relay race, with a balloon on a plate carried round the lines by each child in turn. If the 'jelly' falls off the plate, the 'waiter' has to go back to his place in his own line and start again.

What about a Treasure Hunt? Not everyone approves of mass present-giving at parties. I know of one mother of four who strongly disapproved. She felt she could not possibly afford to give presents at her children's parties. So she gave no parties, and consistently declined all invitations as well. One admires such firm sticking to principles; and it is true that a custom of elaborate present-giving can become an abuse and may indeed discourage people of slender means from giving parties at all.

But on the whole I think it a good custom especially on birthdays when guests are likely to bring presents themselves. It is good for the 'birthday girl' or boy to give as well as to receive. The presents certainly need not be expensive. A toy costing a few shillings, if chosen cleverly, is just as likely to please as one costing twice as much. Plastic toys, crayons, pencils, beads, painting-books, all are still cheap. And the birthday child or Christmas hostess loves wrapping them up and labelling them.

When it comes to hiding the treasures, let your child do it. She is more likely than you are to remember where they are hidden. At one party I attended a small boy had to go home without his treasure. Neither guests nor hostess could find it!

On several birthdays, feeling we needed a change from the usual hunt, we dressed Judith and Rachel up as gipsies. They sat in a tent made of bedspreads, and the children visited them one after another to have their fortunes told and a parcel pressed into their hands. Some of the little ones found it a trifle awe-inspiring.

Parties should end with a cooling-off, both physical and emotional. It is wise to choose a less riotous game, like General Post, towards the end, rather than finish up as at Hunt Balls with a gallop.

As for the cooling drinks, don't leave them till the first batch of parents arrive, or you may forget them altogether. One Christmas our last guests had departed before I remembered the fridge was still stiff with ices.

A last word to the adult hostess. It is your job to help your child guests make a polite exit. So make yourself conspicuous. They've been told to thank you, but they don't always know which one is *you*! Particularly if you have a large 'staff' of grown-up helpers. 'Oh, I thought she was Jane's mother,' whispers Five-year-old, after a bad shot.

Another fault in hostesses is not noticing a proferred hand or not hearing the low murmur of a three-year-old, repeated more than once, '… and thank you very much for having me'. The Mamas, released at last from their arduous duties, chat gaily together, and in the end the unnoticed child gives up and goes home without saying goodbye.

And you say afterwards, 'Children have no manners these days …' Parties always raise that manners problem. So in the next chapter the question shall be squarely put. What are good manners?

11

What Are Good Manners?

I must make one thing clear at the start. I am strongly in favour of civilised behaviour—both in children and adults. We all like children who are polite to us. And children like adults who are polite to *them*. So in any discussion of children's manners the first point must be: Parents, remember your own 'please' and 'thank-you'. There must be an end to the abrupt and dictatorial, 'Post this letter …' 'Open the door… .'

Now for the children's attitude towards manners. In my experience children are not against manners *as such*. It is no more trouble for them to say 'Please' than it is to say 'Bags I' or 'Gimme'. In fact, 'please' is such a short and modest little monosyllable it is hard to see at first why it should be such a trouble-maker.

The difficulty about 'please' is not in itself, but in its associations. Children instinctively feel it is part of the grown-up game. Part of adult technique. Of civilisation. And they react against being pressed into that mould too soon. Their natural impulse is to cling on to their pre-civilised state as long as possible. Hence the sometimes deliberate refusal to learn manners. Many a mother has exclaimed in exasperation 'When will you learn your manners?' The real question is when the child will choose to employ manners which he has learnt long ago and knows perfectly well. A mother from Worksop, Notts., reports chronic 'if you please' trouble, ending in her small daughter's triumph. 'When she asked for a biscuit one day, I said, "If you what?" The answer was, "If you fetch it".' Of course children sometimes genuinely forget to say the magic word. But more often than not it is a case of remembering to forget.

The fact that children connect good manners with an adult mode of life is frequently shown in their imaginative games. Two parents, one from Somerset and one from Cheltenham, describe how their children, when acting the part of *adults* in make-believe games, laid great stress on the importance of good manners. 'My adopted daughter,' writes one, 'had two little imaginary boys to whom she gave the names of Croddick and David. They were dressed in their prettiest clothes and taken to parties. During the drive home, the law was laid down to them about their "please" and "thank-yous".'

The other tells how her daughter Elizabeth, between two and five, had two imaginary adult friends, Mrs Bonzing and Mrs Sparing. She treated these two with all the politeness due from one grown-up to another. 'The ladies were frequent visitors at our home, and Elizabeth's manners were always quite perfect. "Do come in and sit down—will you stay to tea with us?"'

These stories show that a child expects grown-ups to train children in manners, and also expects adults to show good manners towards each other. But this expectation on the part of our children does not prevent them from reacting unfavourably to the training itself.

How can we help our children to absorb good manners naturally, so that they become part of their own pattern of living, and not something artificially attached to them or even imposed upon them by an alien world? We want to avoid both open revolt and inner friction. The one is painful for us; the other for them. In neither state will they achieve true good manners—manners which express their own civilised attitude to life.

Personal example, as we saw at the beginning of the chapter, is the surest way of all to help them. Whatever we are training our children for—whether it be to be clean, mannerly or moral—example is always a hundred times stronger than precept. For children are consummate imitators.

Another way of helping them is again a question of action rather than words. Encourage them to go places where they will naturally and without too much conscious effort be on their best behaviour.

Do not be nervous that because they are often unmannerly at home they will behave like hooligans whenever they are not under your reproving eye. Let them find themselves as frequently as possible in situations where they will want to behave in a civilised way. Charity begins at home. Good manners often begin outside it. At least, that is where they first become visible. The seed will have been sown at home.

The father of a large family in Leeds who had not found the training of his children an altogether smooth or satisfactory affair, wrote to describe one aspect of their behaviour which gave him cause for pride. 'In our street a generous young couple entertain all the children to TV. My youngsters sit in a row in front of the screen, all ears and eyes. The youngest sits on his knee. This friend says all my youngsters are exceedingly quiet and well-behaved children, which to us parents is as good as the George Cross at any investiture.'

Temporary Lapses

Parents sometimes find that a child whom they have regarded as well-trained in ordinary good manners will suddenly appear to lapse into completely uncivilised behaviour. This may be very distressing unless the shocked and disappointed parent realises that there is some valid reason for this sudden decline. Any change in your home life, or disturbance of the child's emotional life, is likely to have the effect of disrupting his manners. Manners, like other forms of training, grow gradually as part of the general routine. They will probably return when there is a settled routine again. That is why so many children seem to behave badly when we take them away on holiday—just when we hope they will show their best manners—and are perfectly 'good' again when we get them home.

A farmer's wife from Wales moved house and took a long time to unpack and resettle all her belongings. 'Meanwhile my little girl,' she writes, 'got so that she was losing all her nice manners. One day I said in a cross voice, "Jennifer, wherever are your manners these days?" Came a swift reply, "Oh, I haven't unpacked them yet!"'

In teaching children manners make sure they really understand what you mean. Manners, though they are not on the same level as etiquette, are somewhat akin to it. For in one sense they are artificial. They are conventions. Or rather, the underlying realities which good manners express are represented in conventional ways. Nothing is so easy to misunderstand as a convention.

A Sussex mother gives an example of how a young child can completely fail to grasp the implications of the kind of language adults tend to use in teaching children manners. 'I was very cross with my daughter over her behaviour. I said, "You must be more reserved." "Very well," she replied, "I'll be like the seats in the theatre. They're reserved."'

Another child was overheard saying to a small friend while playing at grown-up tea-parties, 'Don't talk properly, talk nicely.'

Antonia, at the age of three, helped me to entertain a clergyman who was paying us a call. When he rose to take his departure she said graciously, 'Good-bye, my love.'

But though our national ideas of good manners are conventions—Frenchmen kiss, Englishmen shake hands—they are founded on something real. We should teach our children early about the realities. Good manners, we can explain, are based on consideration for others. To surrender your seat on a bus to an older person is not mere convention. It is real kindness.

Parents are sometimes involved in embarrassing scenes through their children not seeing the point of conventions which to them appear irksome or even cruel. A mother who found herself on a crowded London bus during the rush hour with her small son of six or seven was forced to teach him the elements of 'travel manners' in those most unpropitious circumstances. The child whined and grizzled because he could not have a seat, complaining that his legs were aching and he could not stand up any longer. His mother explained with great patience that many others beside himself were forced to stand and that there was no seat for him. He did not listen, but kept up a more and more angry wail, 'I want to sit down. I want to sit down.' At last a passenger got off the bus and a seat became vacant. An elderly woman sat down in it. The child's rage and self-pity knew no bounds. His whines rose to a yell. Out of pity for the mother another passenger offered him her seat. But his mother bravely refused, saying, 'No, he simply must learn.' This third blow, 'the most unkindest cut of all', was more than flesh and blood could bear. He bawled. For the sake of all, his mother took him off at the next stop.

One must face the fact that there is no fool-proof answer to a situation such as this. Once that painful set of circumstances had developed it was bound to run a painful course, in one way or another. It is not possible to teach such an intangible and complex thing as good manners in the heat of conflict and distress. Therefore, when small children are going to be taken by bus or train, it will save us and them a lot of misery if we give them an idea of what to expect before they start. Before a train journey, for instance, say: 'You will be able to look out of the window if you get a corner seat, or if you stand in the corridor. Mummy will ask the other passengers if they mind the window open a little. It isn't ours to open or shut just as we like. If you want to stand in the corridor you must not keep coming in and out of the carriage. It's very irritating for the other passengers.'

The Meaning of Manners

So far I have only considered the comparatively easy problem of teaching children the meaning of manners which are based on true consideration for other people. But not all good manners are so obviously explicable. What about such apparent frills of civilisation as raising your cap or hat in the street, or passing the sugar to your neighbour before helping yourself? If you take the sugar first yourself it saves time, and only one person has to pass it instead of two. What good does the hat-raising convention do to anybody? How shall we explain these things to the logical child?

The answer lies partly in the fact that children, as well as being logical, are also capable to a truly marvellous degree of understanding the meaning and value of symbols. Indeed, the average child uses symbols far more extensively in his life and growth than do most grown ups. Our failure to understand the necessary place of symbols in all human life is at the root of much of our modern malaise. The child is less likely to query symbolic conventions, once he knows they are real symbols, than his father is. So tell him what the act of hat-raising means and how it grew up. Show him that all these little acts of conventional courtesy are symbols of our respect for others and are not intended to give people physical relief, like the surrendered seat on the bus.

Another approach to this problem is through the child's aesthetic sense—his feeling for beauty, pattern and design. With his acute perception of design in all its forms a child is well able to appreciate the need for a 'design for living'. Try giving him a simple illustration. There is probably a polished table in your house. It takes time, polishing it? It costs money. Yet the table would be just as useful without that glass. Then why polish it? Because it is more attractive that way. Manners give a polish to life.

A word of warning to end with. There is one kind of manners which we are apt to over-emphasise. Table-manners. Meals are a great temptation to parents. The children cannot escape. There they are, seated round the table for a solid half-hour. It seems a golden opportunity to train them in one brand of good manners at least. To see that they do not dawdle, to insist on quiet voices, or better still, no talking at all till the plate is cleared! Our family butter-dish bears the inscription: 'Say little but think much.' (Kevin amended it to 'Say little but eat much'.)

But it is a temptation that must be resisted. Constant correction can ruin a meal just as effectively as bad manners allowed to run riot. Conversation is reduced to a machine-gun fire of do's and don'ts: 'Sit up. Elbows off the table. Don't put your knife in your mouth. Hold your spoon properly. Don't breathe into your glass. Don't talk with your mouth full. Don't eat with your mouth open. Wipe your fingers on your napkin, not on your pants or the chair. Use one hand to hold your bread-and-butter.' The commands are endless, if your aim is to achieve perfect manners. Table-manners will soon kill table-talk, and family meals will become an orgy of nagging.

In discussing the meaning of true good manners we might perhaps remember a certain old rhyme of our childhood days.

> The child that is born on the Sabbath day,
> Is bonny and blithe, and good and gay.

That is the kind of child we say has 'natural good manners'. Gaiety and spontaneity, friendliness and naturalness; these are all important ingredients of true good manners. So try not to drive out your child's 'blithe spirit' by too grim a determination to achieve perfect politeness all at once.

12

Obedience

If a child could look ahead, what a big slice of his life would seem to be taken up with obedience! We obey our parents. Obey our (dare I breathe it?) husbands. Obey (of course) our wives. Obey the law. Obey our consciences. Perhaps a child would not think this slice of life very appetising or the easiest to digest. So how can we help our children to absorb it naturally?

In the case of small children, parents will make life easier for themselves and their toddlers if they remember one rule. In matters of obedience try to avoid a head-on collision of wills. Suppose your toddler seizes his sister's doll. Don't shout, 'Give it back at once, or I'll . . . ' Deflect his attention from the doll by quickly offering him something else you know will attract him. After all, to want to play with his sister's toys is not in itself a crime. If you can suggest an alternative game for that tiresome little brother, and so avoid involving him in a serious battle with his parent's commands and his own desires, you will be achieving success. It is wrong when we are training small children to make every issue, however trivial, into a high question of principle.

The method of *deflection*—of distracting the toddler from his proposed course rather than involving him in possible disobedience—is always worthy of trial, but its success depends a good deal on the disposition of the child himself. With some of my children, for instance, I have found it work admirably; with others, not at all. Antonia was always eager and delighted to be deflected from one activity to another. But when I tried the same dodge on Thomas it failed dismally. The idea of being stopped from doing something he wanted to do made him mad. The proferring of an alternative made him madder still. So be guided by your own individual child.

Deflection, of course, does not in itself teach a child obedience. It simply helps the parent to establish happy relations and to avoid unnecessary causes of conflict. But there is need, even from the earliest years, to begin teaching obedience itself. What are the best ways of doing this?

Once more, it is always a good thing to avoid collisions wherever possible. This is not just for the sake of a quiet life. But because a child's impulse to obey should eventually spring naturally from within himself. We want our children to obey us with less and less of an effort as they grow older. We want them to feel that each act of obedience is in line with their own inner will, as well as with an external command.

Today I sent Michael and Catherine upstairs to make their beds. Michael, the older by two-and-a-half years, was well aware that bed-making was one of his jobs. He could look ahead to bedtime, ten hours away, and envisage the boredom of having to make it then, when he was sleepy and tired, if he did not make it now. If he had remembered he would have made his bed of his own free will without waiting for me to tell him to do so. Result: he went up at once, the model of perfect obedience!

Catherine, on the other hand, had not lived long enough to size up and understand the family situation over bed-making. Even if she remembered the rule, she was probably secretly counting on someone else making the bed for her, if she waited long enough. She was still too young to look ten hours ahead. In so far as she did so, she just had a vague hope that something would turn up in the meantime, to save her the trouble. Her inner will was not in line with my order. Result: she did not obey, but went upstairs and played with her dolls instead.

How can we make our children feel willing to co-operate whenever we call for an act of obedience? We must begin by summoning to our aid the child's own powers of understanding and intelligence.

A child who understands the 'why' finds it easier to obey than one who can see no sensible reason for what he is asked to do. Avoid that peremptory 'Do as you're told', followed, when the child responds with the inevitable 'Why should I?' with an even more peremptory, 'Because I say so!'

That does not mean you must give a reason for every single thing you tell your child to do. But it is certainly wise to make sure that he understands the reasons for the most common commands he is likely to get throughout the day. Take shutting the door, for instance. I myself detest reading or working in a room with the door open. But few children notice whether it is open or shut, and certainly do not mind in the least which it is. Thus it is necessary for most parents to train their children to shut the door when they go out of a room. It is a social habit that will not develop naturally. But in the course of their training you should explain to them why you want it shut—that you are susceptible to draughts and to outside noises, that an open door gives you a feeling of bleakness as if you were sitting in a waiting-room, while a closed door makes you feel cosy and content. Once the explanation has been made, the reason given, there is no need to keep on repeating it. 'Shut the door, please,' is then quite enough.

Reasoning and the use of logical argument in persuading children to obey us is of course a game that two can play. There is no guarantee that bright children will not cap their parents' reasons for doing as they say with even better reasons of their own for not doing so! The wife of a Scottish schoolmaster sends a good example of this:

'My husband sat down at the end of a hard day's work, fagged out. Rosemary, aged four, bursting with energy, said, "Come on, Daddy, let's play horses." I replied, "No, leave Daddy. He's so tired, and not feeling very well." She immediately answered, "Let's play hospitals, then."'

This was a victory for the child's logic. However, it is no bad thing when our children occasionally defeat us in a battle of wits, and a compromise is generally possible. I expect Rosemary and her father were both quite happy to play at Nurse putting her patient to rest.

Instant Obedience

Even if the child accepts your reasons and obeys you, you must not imagine your job is done. Obedience in response to a reasonable explanation is fine in its way, but it is not enough. There are times when *instant obedience*—blind obedience—is vital. 'Theirs not to reason why' is still sometimes relevant even today.

Suppose a sudden danger confronts your child. There's no time to explain what it is. You just shout 'Stop!' or 'Come back!' He must obey automatically. How is it possible to teach this complete obedience, this immediate response to a special note of authority or urgency in your voice? The secret lies in developing a state of trust and confidence between yourself and your child. Ultimately the whole of obedience depends on building up this habit of trust.

Ninety-nine times your child has found you had good reasons for what you asked him to do. Now comes the hundredth time. Obedience is demanded without any reason being given. But by now the child has come to realise that you never ask him to do anything without good cause. Subconsciously he feels that this time, too, there is a good reason for what you say. He trusts you—and obeys.

The Teenager

The teens present a new challenge. Parents must work out new techniques for dealing with the older child. Some of these will be discussed in a later chapter. But as far as obedience is concerned, the problem of how to handle them becomes less and less one of obedience and more and more one of showing interest and sympathy, so that they themselves will be willing for their parents to exert control—even if it is now a somewhat remote control—over them.

Nor is his parents' own change of attitude the only thing which should help the teenager to accept parental advice without feeling he is being humiliated by doing so. As he grows up the boy or girl will make new discoveries about freedom and independence, obedience and authority. He will begin to see the whole problem in proportion, in a wider setting.

He will discover that neither he nor anyone else can ever catch up with that elusive will-o'-the-wisp, absolute freedom. Perhaps when he was ten or eleven he dreamed of a time when he would be his own master, absolutely free to do as he liked. But by sixteen he begins to suspect that dream will never be realised, and in any case was valueless. He will still have to obey somebody or something however old he gets. And when all the world is in the same boat, why worry?

One keen young observer spotted this fact of life at the age of seven. A grandmother records the following dialogue between her grandson and his mother: '*Nigel's Mother*: You must do as you are told until you are twenty-one. Then you will be grown-up, and able to decide for yourself. *Nigel*: Is Grandpa twenty-one? *Mother*: Oh yes, he's over twenty-one. *Nigel*: Well, he still has to do as Grandma tells him.'

Obedience, the child gradually realises, is not reserved, like the local Recreation Ground, 'for children under 14 only'. It is woven into the whole of life. Indeed it is part of man's deepest nature both to give and to exact obedience. Let that be a comfort to the young rebel.

That, and the fact that Man, the Lord and Master, has not yet made even the inanimate universe obedient to his will. The common cold will not knuckle under; any more than the waves did to King Canute. Or the general's sword in this mother's story: 'I was trying to teach my son of four obedience, and telling him that if he is told not to do a thing, he must not do it. For example, I said that if a general tells his soldiers not to shoot, they won't shoot. He replied: "I s'pose if he told his sword not to cut, it wouldn't cut!"'

13

The Problem of Punishment

'There will be no punishment in the new nursery.' Thus speaks one of our ultra-modern educationists, who pioneers for absolute freedom for the child. He does not believe in any training of the child at all. Therefore he does not believe in obedience—for there is nothing a child can obey (except for his own impulses). And since disobedience is 'out', out goes punishment too.

Personally I cannot follow him into his *laissez-faire* nursery. For one thing, I do not believe there is happiness in the absolutely 'free' nursery or schoolroom. Children do not want complete freedom. The burden of responsibility, of continually making choices and decisions, is too great for them. No doubt the best of those who believe in this anarchic freedom are successful with the particular children put in their charge. But I believe their success is not due to their theories but to their own personalities. To the fact that they are passionately interested in children, and have a 'way' with them. Though they profess not to believe in 'training', they are actually training the children through their own example—in patience, forbearance, kindliness, tolerance, and many other virtues which these teachers themselves particularly value, and therefore practise towards their pupils.

Training by example is probably the very best way of training children. But is it enough in itself? The greatest teachers of mankind have always set an example of personal goodness to their disciples. But they have also added to their own personal example a fund of verbal teaching and instruction. For us parents the problem is a very simple one. Few of us would feel so confident of the perfection of our own example that we would dare to leave our children with nothing else to guide them. Hardly a day passes when I am not conscious, for instance, of having been unnecessarily cross, hasty or bad-tempered with one or other of my children. That they do in fact follow my example in this respect is only too painfully obvious. Being myself imperfect in practice, I must try to supplement their training through precept. Of course, the precepts will sink in better if my own practice is not in too flagrant contradiction with them.

Once it has been admitted that training of children both by example and precept is necessary, it follows that obedience to that training is necessary too. Obedience, in fact, is itself a virtue—though not one recognised by the 'freedom' school of thought. If obedience is a virtue, disobedience is the opposite. And in the last resort the only way to prevent continued disobedience is punishment. Now for the question which dominates this chapter: What is the best kind of punishment?

Some of the 'good things' in life are obvious; some are rather odd. Obvious are 'a good read' and 'a good rest'. But what about that old favourite 'a good cry'? Odder still is the 'good smacking'. Who is it good for? Child or parent? Those in favour answer, Both. It relieves the parent's outraged feelings. It punishes the child quickly and effectively. Those against say, Neither. I myself belong to the No's. But I could not lay my hand on my heart and say I had never given a slap. The point is whether we do it deliberately, as part of our corrective policy; or impulsively, because we have lost our temper.

Corporal Punishment

Punishment, whether of children or adults, is always a controversial subject. But people really get hot and come to blows—as indeed one might expect—over *corporal punishment*. Corporal punishment can vary immensely. It can range from the appalling hiding given in an uncontrollable rage, about which we read in our papers and shudder, down to the sharp, smart caning on the hand, delivered calmly and without passion of any kind. For the purpose of this discussion I include under the term 'corporal punishment' any form of punishment, however mild, however severe, which involves a blow causing physical pain.

Let us begin by surveying the arguments in favour of corporal punishment. I am bound to admit they are not inconsiderable.

1 It has a long tradition behind it. 'Spare the rod,' says the proverb, 'and spoil the child.' It is a proverb advocating force, not fatherly finger-wagging. The cave-man, I feel sure, cuffed the cave-child. Not for him the more subtle approach of 'No rhino bones for your supper!' Or here is the Ugly Duchess in *Alice in Wonderland*. She knows that children are naughty on purpose—they *want* to make us mad—and the only way to deal with them is a good slap on the appropriate place.

> Speak roughly to your little boy,
> And beat him when he sneezes,
> He only does it to annoy,
> Because he knows it teases.

A mother from Stoke-on-Trent finds that in her small girl's mind the very word 'punishment' implies violence. She defines it as 'punch-meant'.

2 Corporal punishment, it is argued, follows quickly on the offence. Thus the child connects the slap with his misdeed. This is certainly important. One of the difficulties about punishing children, especially young ones, is to make them feel any connection between 'crime' and punishment. If the penalty is separated by some hours or even days from the offence, what happens? The child has long ago forgotten his misdeed and the punishment seems to him unfair and merely vindictive.

If, in fact, a mother does decide upon a firm slap she should deliver it herself while the incident is fresh. On no account should she say, 'Wait till your Dad gets home . . .' A hiding administered in cold blood by a cheerful parent has something horrible about it. It recalls Daniel O'Connell's description of Sir Robert Peel's smile: 'His smile was like the silver plate on a coffin.'

3 Children, it is said, prefer a slap. At any rate, they prefer it to many other unpleasant things. Here's a five-year-old schoolboy from York who disliked school enough to play truant and risk any punishment that might be coming to him. 'About an hour after taking John to school,' writes his mother, 'he returned home again. I said, "Why have you come home?" He replied, "Well, could I have a good smacking and go to bed?"'

Some children do seem to take that slap lightheartedly. They mind it no more than a bear-cub minds being cuffed by its mother when she's just about had enough of its gambols. It is hard to believe that this kind of corporal punishment really causes what the psychologists call a 'psychological trauma'—a wounding of the personality. The little victims of this type of chastisement are even quite ready to cheek the stern parent, to answer him back, as one four-year-old did at the tea-table. 'If you don't behave I shall smack your bottom,' said his mother. 'You can't,' was the answer, 'I'm sitting on it.'

Parents often notice that children themselves smack 'naughty' toys in play. This is claimed to prove that they believe in smacking, and consider it the best and most natural form of punishment. A mother from Exeter tells how she slapped her three-year-old son Bryan on the leg for knocking off the heads of tulips with a stick. She sent him tearfully indoors. 'A few minutes later I heard a smart slap, and peeping in saw Bryan sitting on the floor slapping at his imaginary baby and saying, "You naughty baby, I am very cross." The tone of voice was so like mine. Then in a subdued voice he whispered, "Sorry, I won't do it again." "That's a good baby," came the reply. Up got Bryan and went off to play, quite satisfied justice had been done.'

What does this story prove? It certainly could not be used to prove that children who smack their toys, or imaginary playmates, are necessarily 'quite satisfied that justice has been done'. It may well be that they simply feel satisfied they have imitated Mummy quite perfectly. Children, as we have said before, are the world's best imitators. They copy us exactly. Imitation, in fact, is their method of learning; of picking up all the tricks, customs and deeper attitudes which will finally add up together to what we call adult behaviour.

But because children copy us it does not imply they approve or disapprove of what they copy. An actor can try to be a perfect Shylock or Othello without approving of their behaviour. The play's the thing! The same applies to children. But the position is very different for us adults, the pattern-makers. The child who spanks his naughty teddy and imitates teddy's tears afterwards is simply a technician practising his art as accurately as possible. But his parents are setting him an example which has a moral content for themselves, and later on will have moral implications for the child too. Since they copy us so exactly we should be careful to let children see only our best behaviour. Is a 'good smacking' the best we can do in the way of corrective action?

Arguments Against Corporal Punishment

With some children it is undoubtedly dangerous to invite them to copy grown-ups in inflicting physical pain. The child who slaps his toy one day hits his sister the next. Perhaps a few years later on he's punching younger children at school. Later still he may even be one of the unfortunates who takes to knives and knuckledusters.

Physical pain and punishment has other more remote, unexpected dangers. Sometimes it exerts a strange, contorted influence over certain children. They actually begin to crave for it, to enjoy it. They grow up as those sad psychological 'cases' who are continually in trouble because deep down in themselves they long to be punished.

It may be that most parents when they smack their children for being naughty would feel quite satisfied in their own minds, if they thought about it at all, that their children would *not* in fact grow up to be violent or maladjusted. And of course most of them would be right. But there are two points to remember.

First, it is impossible to know the full potentialities of your child, either for good or bad, when he is in the smacking stage. So you are always taking a risk, however slight.

Second, your example will be followed by other parents. Where your child is immune to any evil effects, others may suffer. If corporal punishment is the rule, we can be pretty sure that out of the millions of parents who do it successfully, there will be some who should never have done it at all. Corporal punishment is undoubtedly a short cut for the parents. It saves hours of tedious reasoning. But the short cut sometimes leads to the wrong road.

Arguments like these will probably sound remote and far-fetched to normal parents. But there are other arguments against corporal punishment which should appeal more widely. Corporal punishment, for instance, is not an appropriate method for dealing with many of children's most common offences. Mary is 'difficult' over her food. She plays about, making castles with the mashed potato, islands with the custard. Will a smack do any good? It will make her cry. No one in tears can eat. So smacking will aggravate Mary's trouble, not cure it.

Or perhaps Mary is given to grizzling. What could be more irritating than that perpetual whine? Out comes the familiar parental command, 'Stop it at once or I'll …' Of course Mary does not stop it, and after a 'good shaking' is found to do no good, a 'good smacking' follows. Result? The grizzle turns into a roar and Mary's last state is worse than her first.

With babies, corporal punishment is absolutely senseless. A baby who is accustomed to associate his mother with love and play takes his first slap as a joke, akin to tickling. He roars with laughter. Suddenly it hurts—not so much his hand as his feelings. He can hardly believe it is *you* who is doing this thing—his mother, the centre of all his love, security and happiness; his whole world. Nor is there any connection in his mind between his 'naughtiness' and the sudden, devastating withdrawal of your love.

Striking children who are in their teens is to my mind an equally dangerous practice. For every case where it may seem to have a good effect, to 'make them see reason', there are a hundred other cases where it definitely injures and insults their developing personalities. Parents' relations with their teenage children are likely to be fairly tricky, however carefully and thoughtfully we handle them. Why make our task more difficult by resorting to such a barbaric thing as violence?

If we definitely rule out babies and teenagers as fit subjects for chastisement—the one group are too young, the other too old—that only leaves some of the middle years as a possible sphere for operations. Many eminent authorities on child up-bringing would even go further, and reduce the middle years themselves to the very short period that ends at school-age. 'Any form of corporal punishment should be over and done with by the age of five and six,' write Dr Spurgeon English and Mrs Constance Foster, in their book, *Fathers Are Parents, Too*. Surely, then, it is not beyond the wit of man to work out some better way of dealing with this short intermediate span than by a method which is never ideal, and may be dangerous?

Before going on to consider the possible alternatives to the spanking, it is as well to mention briefly one further point. What about the effect on *adults* of administering that 'good smacking'? If you strike a child while in a temper, you may not be able to control yourself. You may begin moderately, but as the yells develop and your temper rises you may end by hitting much harder than you intended. After all, physical violence belongs to the realms of man the animal, not man the rational being. Once we release those jungle impulses it is not always so easy to leash them up again. Not everyone can be sure of sticking to a pre-determined scale of 'thus hard and no harder'.

The appalling cases of cruelty to children reported every week in the Press, amply testify to the horrible situations in which human beings may become involved, once they allow the animal to get control of the man. Even though we ourselves feel absolutely confident that such a thing will never, never be our own fate, the question of example again comes in.

Parents should think twice about using methods which though safe in their own hands may prove pernicious in others'. At present there is no strong public opinion against parental spankings. The general feeling is that 'everyone does it'. Only a few cranks and theorists are supposed to be against it. As a mother who herself has often spanked but always regretted it, I would like to see a definite change in public opinion. I should like to see corporal punishment dethroned from its time-honoured position, and regarded more and more as a confession of failure. No longer honoured except in the breach, corporal punishment should be banned absolutely by those who already distrust it.

Even with public opinion in the unsatisfactory state it is today, there is growing up a tacit agreement that at least one does not strike one's erring child in the street or on the bus. When a 'scene' does occasionally occur in public between an exasperated parent and a maddening child, everyone around turns away his head, shocked by the indecent sight of violence in public.

The sooner we all try to behave in the home as most of us do on the bus—angels of patience and restraint under the most acute provocation—the better for all. I believe public opinion is hovering on the verge of that change. What holds most of us back? Simply a feeling that in the last resort there is nothing else quite so good as a 'good smack'.

My advice to other mothers is this. First, take a vow of perpetual abstinence from corporal punishment. Second, sit down and consider the alternatives. But unless you abandon the beating *first*, you will never get far with the second stage. For there is something about physical punishment—its swiftness, briefness, easiness, handiness, apparent naturalness to man (the animal)—that makes it, once it is allowed at all, so often the first, so seldom the last resort.

In the next chapter, having duly taken the vow. I shall consider those alternatives.

14

Rule Without the Rod

Punishing children is not a pretty subject at any time. Even when we have decided against corporal punishment there is still something faintly distasteful about sitting down and solemnly discussing how to *punish* the young by alternative methods. I believe this feeling is not so sentimental and soft as it may appear. It springs from a lurking suspicion at the back of our own minds that we parents are sometimes not above resorting to punishment when none—not even the mildest—is justified.

Accidental Misdeeds

So before we set about thinking out alternative punishments to the old-fashioned slap, let us review some of those occasions when it is right not to punish at all. Take accidents. Your child accidentally jogs the table. Over goes the ink. Your carpet is ruined. So is your temper. Ink and culprit are both 'on the carpet'. But the child thinks, 'How unfair! I didn't mean to do it.'

Now suppose you bear the disaster without punishing? If your child sees you being generous and forbearing instead of, as he thinks, unfair, he will be deeply impressed. He will make a genuine attempt to avoid such accidents in the future. By being 'generous and for-bearing' I do not mean you should allow a child to get away with every accident until he thinks he can ramp about the house as he pleases, treating your possessions with complete lack of consideration. Even a smack is better than no discipline at all.

No, the kind of treatment I suggest is not *laissez-faire* arising out of parental laziness or irresponsibility: but a clear recognition that accidents, and wilful misdeeds or disobedience, are radically different. The second are punishable. The first are not.

One parent who nobly admitted her tendency to get more annoyed over accidents than necessary, tells an illuminating story. She decided, on consideration, to turn over a new leaf as regards these accidents and not to punish her young son except when he really deserved it. The very next day after making this resolution the test came. Three spots of ink were accidentally dropped on the best chair cover. Her son, no doubt expecting the usual storm, was most apologetic. But his mother simply pointed out that he must be more careful another time, adding, 'but as I know it was an accident I shall not say more about it'. The boy looked at her and then said, 'Mummy, why are you kinder than you usually are?'

What a bitter-sweet comment! And one that, in varying forms, has made every parent squirm and smile at some time or other. But it carries a most consoling message. Namely, that any effort we may make to treat our children more fairly will never for a minute escape their attention. Children notice everything. They are on to every change in our behaviour towards them, whether for better or for worse, like a flash of lightning. One great discouragement to turning over a new leaf is the feeling that 'nothing ever really makes any difference'. With children, it always does.

Another point to remember in dealing with accidents is that a small act of carelessness may cause big damage. We parents are too apt to measure the crime by its results. And to punish accordingly. This is all wrong. We should measure by the intention, not the result. During the holidays one of my children picked up a beautiful Chinese porcelain cat belonging to her Granny, to admire its smooth surface and charming expression. But she had been told never to touch Granny's precious china, and was four years old, not a baby. No one saw it happen; but accidentally an ear was chipped off. This was irreparable damage. Never again would it be the perfect cat. Yet the offence was a relatively small act of disobedience. If the ear had not broken off the child's disobedience would probably not have been noticed at all. How many Grannies would have had the good sense, logic and justice to insist on no punishment other than the obvious lesson to be drawn from the incident—that disobedience is a bad thing in itself, and you can never calculate or control its results?

Sometimes a severe accident may cause the parent such distress that the child is bound to notice it. This, in itself, is a kind of punishment. In certain circumstances it is as well to let your child see how upset you are by the damage she has done, even if it is only due to trifling carelessness. But this form of punishment could turn out to be a very harsh one, and must not be overdone. Small children are extremely sensitive to signs of distress on the part of their parents. It tends to make them feel bewildered, frightened and insecure.

If you have on some occasion been unable to control yourself and shown your child the unhappiness she has caused, this is indeed punishment enough. Here is a story from a Hampshire mother to illustrate this point.

'I had left my small daughter in the dining-room for a moment. On returning, I found she had been playing with my best cut-glass wine-glasses, and had broken three of them. I picked her up on my lap to scold, but could not stop my tears from flowing. With her tiny finger she softly pushed one back into my eye.'

One correspondent wrote to say that she felt this 'punishment' was far too severe, even though it was delivered by the unfortunate mother quite unwillingly. 'I am certain anything, slap, rows, or shaking is better for a child than to see his mother weep. . . . Mental cruelty does more damage than a slight bang on the bottom.'

I agree with the second sentence in this letter, but the case of the wine-glass quoted above does not seem to me to qualify even as mild mental cruelty. In fact, it strikes me as a rather touchingly human story. Obviously one should not cry on purpose to punish a child. But when it happens, as on rare occasions it might, unintentionally, the whole situation may be taken as an example of poetic justice. In any case, I see no reason why our children should not realise that parents have emotions like other people. If it is all right to show a child anger, excitement, joy, hope, disappointment, weariness, preoccupation and all the other emotions that crop up inevitably during the day, why not occasionally show sorrow too? I do not believe in the idea of a parent being a carefully controlled semi-automatic unsmiling, unfrowning figure, created for the calm distribution of machine-made justice.

The discussion has led us some distance away from the original question of how to deal with accidents. On this point, my feeling is that all parents tend to punish accidental disaster too severely. Whenever one of those unfortunate episodes occurs always ask yourself first, 'Is a punishment really necessary?'

Often we parents let off our children if the mischief they do happens to make us laugh. Six-year-old Glenys was found one day behind the airing-cupboard door, painting red spots on her blue and white sandals. She already had a red-white-and-blue frock and hair ribbon, so wanted shoes to match. 'It caused too much of a joke for me to scold her,' writes her mother.

How sensible. Yet how illogical! Why only let them off that punishment if we see the joke?

Pathos, as well as pranks, may earn a remittance of punishment. A three-year-old Catford boy moved from a house with a garden into a house with a yard—and petrol drums. He promptly began filling his water-can with petrol and 'watering' his toys. Covered in oil—for he kept on slipping down in the oozy yard—he explained to his mother: 'But Mummy, I was only watering my garden.' 'I could not be cross,' she adds, 'knowing he was missing his garden.'

In each of the cases quoted above the mother quite rightly decides not to be cross. First, because the child makes her laugh. Second, because he makes her sorry for him (of course, unconsciously). But there was a deeper reason common to both cases. The parents were understanding enough to realise that their children had no *intention* of being naughty. And so had no need to be punished. You can always warn children against making a mess in future without punishing them for the first offence. And remember that what seems to you a *second* offence—and therefore punishable—may in the child's mind still be a first offence.

Children are not always able to see that the same principle is involved in what seems to them a totally different situation. They are often tiresomely literal-minded and stick to one's verbal commands. Kevin was told not to draw on his bedroom wall and given a large sheet of paper to perform on instead. Next day I found a number of pencil squirly-wigs on the paint of the staircase. 'Oh *Kevin* …' I began vehemently. 'But you only said I mustn't draw on my bedroom wall,' he protested, quite innocently.

Of course children sometimes use trivial verbal differences as an excuse for doing something they really know quite well is forbidden. Every parent has to apply common sense and his knowledge of his own child, to these instances. The intelligence and age of the child also counts, and many other factors. General rules are no substitute for individual knowledge.

Michael, at nine, knew that he had to change his dirty shoes when he came into the house. If he failed to do so he lost one of his good-night sweets. One day he marched into the drawing-room in a pair of particularly muddy gum boots. 'Oh, but the rule is only about changing *shoes*,' was his hopeful try-on. The look on his face, apart from anything else, made it clear there was not a trace of genuine ignorance this time. He lost his sweet.

Children Can Be Naughty

Above is one instance of a minor offence and a minor punishment. What shall be our rule when a punishment is really necessary? When it is not a question of an accident or a prank or the expression of some inner unhappiness? For children *can* be naughty—though many modern writers would disagree. Unlike the philosopher Rousseau, who is quoted with approval by more than one modern educationist, I believe that babies are born with potentialities both for evil and for good. (Whereas Mr A.S. Neill, for instance, whose views are mentioned elsewhere in this book, says that his own philosophy implies 'a belief in human nature, a belief that there is not, and never was, original sin'. I too have a belief in human nature, but not the same one.)

This does not mean that a baby is capable of naughtiness. He certainly is not. But imperceptibly, between the ages of three and six, we can see it coming. Our own handling of the child will hasten or retard its development. But the seeds of good and evil have always been there.

By the time a child is seven he is a morally responsible being, though a very immature one. It is our duty as parents to train his moral sense. You may still object that training does not imply the need for punishment. We do not punish adults when they fail in their training, whatever it is. We leave it to circumstances to punish them. Then why not just *tell* the child when he has done something wrong, and leave it at that? As when a young man takes an examination and is told he has failed, but is not punished for failing.

The answer is that we assume adults *want* to be trained in whatever they willingly undertake. Therefore their failure will be one of ability, not of will. A child, on the other hand, often very definitely does not want to be trained in the particular way we think he ought. Hence a sanction is necessary; a punishment to persuade him in future to alter his will in the direction we wish.

The words I have used above might give rise to one serious misunderstanding which I will now hasten to undo. The training of children is not, as it may have sounded, just a case of one will against another. Mine against his or hers. If it were no more than this I should feel great sympathy with the school of thought which advocates the absolutely 'free child'. After all, where one will is as good as another, let's support the weaker side!

But the truth is far otherwise. The only reason why parents have a right to train their children is because they are supposed to be teaching them to obey, not their *own* will, but the Moral Law—the will of God. To do Right with a big R not a small one. To 'be good' in an absolute sense, not just good in a sense which happens to be convenient to grown-ups, e.g. sitting still while Mummy is writing a letter. (Though even this superficial form of 'being good' may be part of real training.) If a parent deliberately trains his child against the moral law, he forfeits his right to train at all. Parents who teach their children to shop-lift or receive, have them taken away from them. The training most of us give is a mixture of real morality and our own convenience.

Alternatives to Corporal Punishment

Now at last we are going to look around for the sanctions. You have ruled out a 'good hiding' as a punishment. Try a 'good scolding' instead. A scolding is a verbal assault. Language distinguishes man from the beasts. So a scolding, unlike a beating, does not offend against our dignity as human beings. But as a regular punishment it has its own drawbacks.

Children become immune to scoldings surprisingly quickly. They only have the maximum good effect on two conditions. First, that they are not overworked. Second, that there is a close and happy relationship between yourself and the child. Unless the child values your good opinion of him the scolding will be of little or no use. As soon as the scolding is over—and that should be as soon as possible—change your voice completely and let your child feel he can start afresh again.

Be careful that the business of giving constant scoldings does not have a bad effect upon *you*. A scolding may be like an X-ray. It may cure the 'patient' but injure the 'doctor' who uses it. See that scolding does not turn you into a scold.

If your child reacts to your scolding well, i.e. listens patiently and says he is sorry, you may be tempted to improve the golden hour by extending your rebuke into a sermon. Children detest 'sermonising'. So never throw in general remarks on good behaviour, when it is a case of a particular misdeed. Stick to the point. Be brief. Nothing need be added 'for good measure'.

Turn, now, from the scolding to another favourite form of punishment. Is it permissible to punish children through their stomachs? Yes and No. Never send them supperless to bed, unless they happen to be at the stage where 'supper' is just a treat, and not one of their necessary meals. You would not think of making your child go without a cardigan on a cold day, as a punishment. The same should apply to food, where it is a question of the child's health.

My convictions on this point are strengthened by a note I received from Judith not long ago. Inspired by reading some of my views on children, she decided to send in a few critical remarks about parents. High in the list comes our failure to appreciate the torments of incessant hunger in the young!

'Now for one of my pet complaints against grown-ups. I am nearly always hungry, especially after supper, strange though that seems. The sight of the grown-ups' lovely hot sizzling supper being dished up makes you feel ravenous again, even though you have only just finished your own. Then they call you greedy and wonder how you can fit in another mouthful. They look at you as though you were a man-eating lion or a mammoth.'

Luxury foods are another matter. You can safely deprive them of 'good-night' sweets, lollies, ices, or jam for tea. But do not say 'No sweet tonight' if your three or four-year-old child refuses to eat his toast at eight-o'clock in the morning. The gap in time is too long for him to remember the reason for his punishment. It is not till a child is about six that one can perhaps punish him at the end of the day for something he has done at the beginning. But the shorter the gap, at any age, the better. It is a mistake to think that the punishment should always *fit* the 'crime'; but it should always be *near* it—in time. (Sensible parents will not try to punish unkindness with unkindness, cheating with cheating or a pinch with a pinch.)

One further remark on this aspect of the subject. Unless your child has plenty of small luxuries and treats in his life, you will not be able to use any form of punishment which consists in taking them away. You cannot discipline a child who has no fun.

Does this sound callous? Are we to give a thing with one hand simply in order to be able to take it away with the other? Not at all. The point is that to bring up a child with too much austerity defeats its own end. When, despite his bleak upbringing, he does something wrong, you will find yourself in a dilemma. None of the little pleasures of a child's life will be available whose deprivation makes the convenient mild punishment. Therefore you may be driven into action which is much too drastic.

This is simply another way of saying that punishment only succeeds where the family background is one of love and confidence, fun and games. Where a child knows he is loved through all the ups and downs of life whether he is in disgrace or in favour, your system of correction, provided it is sane and reasonable, is almost sure to work. Even a slapping, though it is a 'low' form of punishment, will probably not harm the normal child.

But once the atmosphere of the home is one of fear and anxiety, almost any punishment is liable to worsen the child's character rather than to reform it. Plenty of fun with the parents, and small treats on however economical a scale, undoubtedly help to build up in the child's mind a feeling that he is loved and appreciated.

Apart from immediate advantages to themselves in disciplining the child, parents are right to plan a family regime in which a system of rewards and punishments has its place. After all, it is our business to prepare our children for the kind of world they are eventually going to enter. The child's home should in one sense be a carefully doctored miniature of the great world—'doctored' because they will be protected against the worst dangers and evils by us until they are fully equipped, from within, to face them. Rewards and punishments are an integral part of 'real life'. Perhaps the most real of all. So we are right to give them a place in our system of training.

The imposing of fines is often a reasonable method of punishment. But here again, the question arises of when to impose them. If the child happens to have some pennies left at the time that he misbehaves, it is all right to fine him. Or if he is naughty fairly near to a Saturday—the day his pocket-money arrives! But if he teases his sister, or makes a row before getting-up time on *Monday* morning—well, you must think of something else. The gap from Monday to next Saturday will be too long.

How about banishment? Sending children to bed or out of the room? Rachel went through a phase at about three of flying into rages during meals. She would be sent out of the room in an apparently distraught condition, and at first would remain weeping outside the door for as long as ten minutes. Suddenly the mood would pass. A face would appear round the door smiling broadly, and Rachel was back among us. Gradually she shortened the period of her exile from ten minutes to five, and then less still. Finally her stay outside was a purely token one. Out she went crying, only to return immediately with a smiling face. The whole thing became a family joke and then died out, the rages with it.

There is no doubt that some children welcome temporary banishment, whether to bed or outside the door. A quiet rest on one's bed often calms a fit of temper. Kevin, when in trouble, instinctively rushes up to his bedroom, throws himself down on his bed, as if on the lap of mother earth, and quickly gets over it.

On the other hand, if you already have 'bedtime' difficulties it is obviously unwise to send your child to bed as a punishment. It will only confirm him in his view that bed is a bad show—a sort of condemned cell. There is always the danger, too, that a small child may fall asleep and upset his proper routine of sleeping and waking. A three-year-old from Acton evidently had some inkling of this kind of situation. This is how his mother writes: 'When I threatened my son aged three that he would be put in his cot as a punishment, he replied, "Then I'll go to sleep and sleep all day and keep you awake all night!"'

Three General Rules

Here are three rules for reprimand, to wind up with.

1 Never threaten a punishment you do not intend to or cannot perform. Empty threats are spotted immediately by children, and punishment becomes a mockery. 'If you don't behave I shall leave you behind when we all go to the cinema.' The child knows perfectly well you do not intend to leave him alone in the house, and your empty threat passes over his head.

Perhaps the favourite among empty threats is the threat of desertion if a child is not good. Mothers, goaded beyond endurance, are far too fond of throwing out this terrific warning. But to the normal happy child it is not terrific at all. It is just a meaningless form of words. Here are two instances where the children's casual, matter-of-fact reception of this threat-to-end-all-threats showed that they took it with more than a pinch of salt.

A South Shields father writes: 'Maurice had been very trying that morning. In desperation Mother exclaimed, "I will run away and leave you." After a moment Maurice asked, "Who will cook we's dinners?"' What a molehill of a reaction to a mountainous threat!

And here is a Lincoln mother who tried the same tactics with Raymond, aged four. 'I said, "You are a naughty boy, Raymond. I will run away and leave you." Quite unconcerned he replied, "Take me with you, then." I smile to myself over that incident now, for it is my son who is miles away from me—emigrated to Australia.'

It is indeed a blessing that the normal child frankly disbelieves this kind of threat. If he did believe it, how devastating it would be to his feelings of security in his home. A *cri de coeur* comes from a correspondent, now a mother herself, who has never forgotten the agony which threats of desertion caused her when she was young. 'The child of divorced parents, I never knew with whom I was to spend the holidays. I can remember writing home from school to an aged aunt, who last holidays had said she would disown me: "I presume I am now the property of Captain X . . . "'

2 Never inflict punishment without warning. Always say '*Next time* you do that I'll . . .' Children are often quite genuinely unaware of whether a certain type of behaviour would be condemned as naughty or not. To take a trivial instance. Most small children discover sooner or later the joys of bubbling in their milk. They begin to bubble softly, then louder, and finally, with a great spluttering and splashing, they choke. Don't say in a horrified voice, 'Leave the table at once!' Give them a warning that this is not the way to behave and if they do it again they will have to go away.

Of course children will tend to take advantage of this scrupulous fairness. But never mind. Don't feel you must score every point. Your authority should be strong enough to take an occasional verbal defeat. Catherine, at seven, suddenly picked up her plate at lunch and began licking it like a dog. I told her to leave the table. 'Oh,' she protested, 'you never said I couldn't do it!'

3 If *next time* comes, be sure to carry out the punishment. A parent who is all bark and no bite might as well abdicate. It is better not to threaten at all than to keep on threatening and never act. Such a system, or lack of system, has every disadvantage. It prevents you ever training your children effectively, without at the same time creating a happy atmosphere. For threats are always flying about and the children have an uneasy fear that some time they might even be fulfilled! In this one respect the training of small children resembles the training of young animals. It must be consistent.

15

'He's So Rough ...'

'I want to kill somepin'! I want to kill somepin'!' With a thrill of horror I realised this was my eldest son Thomas, aged three, strutting about the house brandishing a stick. Are these the first dreaded signs of a juvenile delinquent, I wondered? Visions of visits to child guidance clinics floated before me.

Kevin, at six years old, loves to tussle and fight like a puppy. But Catherine, though taller and stronger, is most unwilling to oblige as a sparring partner. The other day I suggested he should pummel the old, sofa instead. He went at it with a will for ten minutes. Later that day he said darkly, 'My job is to be naughty... .' 'Why, Kevin?' 'Because I want to punch Catherine.' 'Didn't the old sofa do?' 'No. I want to hear it scream.'

Many parents experience doubts as their angelic toddler grows into a 'real boy'. A bit too much of a real boy, they begin to suspect. Physical violence is now his favourite pastime. He won't play with farmyard animals any more. He only wants guns and soldiers. One tries to tempt him with something at least one degree removed from the real thing; perhaps medieval knights in silver armour, or harmless Yeomen of the Guard. But no. Even the scarlet Coldstreams are only his second choice. Plain khaki is first favourite! The innocent prattle of babyhood has disappeared too. Now his chief utterances are rapid machine-gun fire and exploding bombs.

I gave Thomas a box of crayons. He used them as 'ammo'; pointed them at me shouting bang! bang! bang! Ought I to have banished all those marching men and Bren-gun carriers long ago? Replaced them by timber-wagons and rows of lead hens?

I am glad now that I did not. Ten years later the same child had become an arch-humanitarian. When the rest of us went to the Zoo he refused to come 'because it's cruel to shut up wild animals'. For a time circuses, too, came under the ban, and of course 'blood sports'. His early bellicosity had in fact been the expression of a childish love of adventure. A desire to sound 'big'. It did not indicate cruelty.

A friend of mine, however, took the opposite line. She dreaded the effect of 'war toys' on her son. Not a single soldier was allowed to pollute his nursery. Result? He developed a secret craving for them. One day he went to a children's party. His roving eye spotted a box of the forbidden fruit—soldiers. He carried them furtively into a corner. Like a miser, he gloated over his treasure all through the party, guiltily satisfying his thwarted longing.

Personally, I am no longer anxious when my younger sons play 'Battles' with all the ghastly realism at their command—though I still shrink, from an aesthetic point of view, from the moment when a death-wound is received, with its accompanying gurgles and writhing and clutching, copied very accurately from the cinema.

At this age boys' violence is usually due to a vivid imagination and high spirits, not to innate depravity. A mother from Guernsey tells the following anecdote, which illustrates my point.

'I was taking my two children for a walk along a London street. Some argument was going on as to who should walk on the kerb. Both children wanted to. The girl, aged six-and-a-half, was inclined to domineer over the boy, a very gentle child of five. Of course she got her way. Suddenly, to my horror, the boy turned on her and knocked her down! I started to give him a good scolding. He interrupted me to explain patiently: "But, Mummy, I felt like a Knight in Shining Armour!"'

While his mother was right to explain that knights made a point of rescuing ladies not bowling them over, she was also right to regard this incident as dramatic rather than sinister. Small boys who do battle in the world of their imagination should not cause their parents undue anxiety, even when a sudden tide of emotion carries them into unexpected violence. The time for careful watching of our sons is not three or five but thirteen and fifteen.

The instinct for adventure and glory may be perverted if the teenager joins a 'gang'. He may do violent acts to impress his leader, or his girl—a thoroughly dangerous situation. But even at this age we must be guided by the boy's whole character and behaviour rather than by any apparently disconcerting externals. Love of fire-arms, for instance. In a recent tragic case it was noticed that a young criminal had always shown 'an unhealthy interest in fire-arms'; and in this he had been encouraged by his father. But with a boy otherwise normal, interest in fire-arms may be perfectly normal too.

Thomas, even at the height of his 'anti-blood-sport' phase, was still fascinated by the noise and smoke of lethal weapons. After the passion for an air-gun had been satisfied and died, various swoppings at school brought a number of exotic pistols into his possession; and a small brass cannon was constructed under a schoolmaster's guidance, that now and then succeeded in blowing itself to pieces in a far corner of the sports ground. I believe the last additions to his lethal family were a pair of ancient duelling pistols, dug out of an ancestral treasure-chest. I remember the police kindly said that they need not be licensed on the grounds that they would never fire again. But somehow they were persuaded to put up one last show, and I remember the deafening explosion as they riddled a row of treacle tins in the sand-pit.

The love of a bang, from firework or gun, seems to be deeply rooted in boys. There is something picturesque, rollicking, even funny about it, which appeals to them. Of course such things are dangerous. But dangerous to possible companions, rather than to the marksman's own character. (I always insisted on these things being done alone, or under strict adult supervision.) Therefore I do not think it wise to suppress these instincts in a boy's early life, as long as he is not bullying others.

It would be wrong to go away with the idea that only boys have aggressive instincts in childhood. They seem to be just as common in girls at a certain stage, though not so obvious because not expressed systematically and elaborately in games like soldiers.

When Antonia was about a year old a cousin, a few months older, came to stay with us. I put them both into the pram, one at each end, and took them for a walk. Antonia was thrilled by the visitor, offering her toys and showing every sign of delight. Suddenly she bent down and buried her teeth (luckily not very many!) in her cousin's bare leg.

Several years later I noticed that Rachel, at the age of two had developed the same trick. Extremely affectionate, when carried against one's shoulder she would kiss it one minute and bite it the next. People used to say she was trying out her new teeth, like a cat sharpening its claws. In reality, it was due to the intensity of emotion a small child feels quite suddenly and can neither control nor understand. Violent love, the pure violence into which it turns, and the love which quickly returns—these all chase each other through the child's heart and mind. At first it is disconcerting. But it is a stage that is quickly outgrown and on no account should be taken to indicate the beginnings of a bad character. Never 'teach the child what it feels like' by biting back, as some misguided people do. I can testify that the chief biter in my family is growing up rather more placid and serene than her brothers and sisters!

Talking of growing out of things, it may be a consolation to other parents to know that violent phases in play and phantasy, if not thwarted, are often of fairly short duration—though of course they may recur at intervals. Parents who are heartily sick of the sound of aeroplanes dropping bricks on toy soldiers' heads, can look forward to the time when this particular game will suddenly be dropped. After a visit to a friend who had a fine clockwork train set, Kevin switched dramatically and completely from battles to transport. For the next birthdays and Christmas we were asked for nothing but trains. It was such a relief to buy nice little boxes marked 'Railway Staff' and 'Passengers' instead of the eternal searchlights and A.A. guns. But of course the noise had to go on. For the same instinct that revels in a battle makes sure that no train gets round the circuit too often without a major accident.

Aggression Due to Unhappiness

There is, however, another kind of violence in children which may really indicate some unhappiness or maladjustment in their lives. This type of aggressiveness must be recognised as such, and not just put down to pent-up energy. It may not be serious enough to necessitate a resort to expert guidance (though this may occur if it is not recognised in time and is allowed to increase). It generally means that the parents should realise their child is disturbed about something, and should find out what it is and try to dispel it.

Here is a story from Sussex, light-hearted and non-serious in itself, which indicates the way these things may happen. The mother, though she laughed afterwards, was quite shaken at the time.

'I walked into the pantry one morning with my little girl aged six. Brian, her two-year-old brother, banged the door on us, and as the catch was on the outside, we were shut in. He went off to play, ignoring our appeals to climb on a chair and open it. Through the small window we could see him calmly playing in the garden with his little spade. After some time a neighbour heard our knocking and released us. It had been a most uncomfortable experience. The two of us together hardly had room to turn round. I was so relieved to be let out at last that I forgot to scold him.' Which I feel sure was just as well. For I strongly suspect that this 'act of aggression' on Brian's part was caused by jealousy of his older sister. By 'putting her in prison' he was asserting his power over her. Once she and her mother were safely behind bars, he was king—a vagabond king, it is true, but that is better than being a younger brother. Like Alexander Selkirk digging on his desert island he can feel at last 'I am monarch of all I survey'.

One final story, this time about two small brothers. Peter is three and Nicholas not yet two. Peter's parents have noticed for some time that he is becoming extremely hostile towards his baby brother. He goes about the house muttering. 'Horrid Nicholas. Horrid Nicholas. Horrid Nicholas.' His Godfather pays him a visit and decides to tackle this ugly situation before it gets any worse. He says to Peter: 'I am very old. I am so old that I have learnt how to see right into people's hearts. I can see into your heart, Peter. Do you know that your *heart* is not saying "Horrid Nicholas"? It is only your *lips* that are saying it.' Next day Peter is heard muttering—but with a difference:'Horrid Nicholas. I only say it with my lips …'

Jealousy is behind many a feeling of aggression and violence in the child's world, as in the world of adults. In the next chapter the monster must be dragged into the open.

16

Jealousy

When we have a bout of reckless extravagance we may feel fine—at least for a time. When we indulge our pride we may get quite a kick out of it. But jealousy seems to be a vice on its own. To feel jealous is to feel miserable. It brings its own immediate punishment. That is one reason why we should never punish our children for their jealous scenes. Our job as parents is to cure jealousy if it's there, and prevent it developing when we suspect it's likely to grow.

In this chapter I shall deal only with a few examples of jealousy. For it is a hundred-headed monster as well as being 'green-eyed'. But if we can cut off a few of the heads, unlike the monster's in the legend they will not grow again. And we shall send our children out into the world fortified against the most hateful form of self-torture they will ever know.

The Displaced Baby and the New Baby

When my son arrived a short time after his elder sister I was prepared for trouble. Trouble due to jealousy on the part of the ex-baby towards the interloper. But I frankly did not expect anything very serious. For had I not read the right books, studied the psychiatrists, found out exactly how to cope? First, I had prepared my daughter well beforehand for the new arrival. Then, on the first day I gave the baby his bath, I was careful to invite his sister to attend. He was to be 'her baby' as well as mine. She should always help me with him. Thus her natural jealousy would be swallowed up in her love, care and interest.

Alas, in less than a minute she had seized the soap-dish and dealt him a shrewd blow on the head. Next day I heard the baby crying in the nursery. Suddenly his normal wailing turned to strange stifled sounds. I ran in. There he was, buried at the bottom of his cot under a pile of his sister's toys. Dolls, balls, bricks, a china tea-set—anything to obliterate him completely.

My husband and I were never able to agree on the exact interpretation of her drastic action. He, ever charitable, thought she was loading him with her toys to cheer him up and stop him crying. I feared the crying had got on her nerves and she was trying to silence him for her under the 'lid' of toys. But we both realised a toddler's reactions to the new baby are something to be reckoned with. You cannot just smooth them away by inviting Two-year-old to co-operate.

A letter from a Glamorgan mother paints an even more startling picture of a child's ruthless logic in his attitude towards new-comers in the family circle.

'Three kittens were born on a Saturday and two had to be drowned. My five-year-old son asked his father why he drowned two and kept one. "So that the mother cat will not pine for the two lost ones," his father replied. On the Monday following his mother had triplets, two girls and a boy. His Dad took the boy in to see the new arrivals, on which the boy said, "Which of those are you going to drown, Dad? Drown the girls and keep the boy for a brother for me."'

It is unwise to assume that every child will spontaneously feel love for a new-born, provided he is not jealous of it. Some children are as indifferent or allergic to babies as many grown ups are. A boy of seven was taken to see a week-old cousin and asked what he thought of her. 'I can't like her,' he replied; 'she has such a selfish look on her face.' We mothers take for granted that special look of infinitely remote, almost Chinese detachment on the wise little features of a new-born baby. To a child, who likes a responsive expression, the new-born look is not attractive.

When my son Thomas was in turn displaced by a younger brother his reaction was no more favourable than his elder sister's had been to himself. 'What shall we call the baby?' I asked him, again trying to make the ex-baby take an active interest in the new-comer. 'Nothing,' was the prompt answer. 'Oh, but he must have a name.' 'Well, call him Tom. It's a little *bother* of a name.' Thomas, in choosing an abbreviated form of his own name, clearly showed his opinion of the baby. It was going to be a small, tiresome replica and rival of himself.

The truth, of course, is that toddlers vary as much in their likes and dislikes as do mature human beings. The only safe rule is: Study your individual child. Some will love the new baby, especially if they are allowed to feel it is theirs. Others will be bored by it whatever you do. And more bored the more you try to force its charms on them. If your toddler finds the new baby uninteresting and even irritating, respect his feelings. Speak of the new baby matter-of-factly when you have to refer to it. Don't wax lyrical and begin murmuring 'Isn't she *sweet*?' At the same time, pay more attention to the toddler than usual. He will be just the age when he wants to play games with you. Be at his service. Read to him. Do cut-outs with him. Make him feel that life after the baby's arrival is even more fun than it was before.

Do not, if you can possibly avoid it, send him off to nursery school the moment the baby is born. You may feel you need and deserve the extra hours of peace. You may even feel convinced your toddler is perfectly happy at school. But it is almost certain that you will have fixed indelibly in his mind a disastrous pattern of cause and effect. He will feel, without any doubt, that baby's arrival drove him from home. Even if he likes being away he won't like the feeling of being driven out. And he won't like the baby who drove him. In the end you will find you have less peace at home instead of more. For the first reaction of the banished toddler will be to become perfectly unmanageable the moment he gets home again. If it is necessary for him to go to a nursery school it is much better to wait till a few months after the baby's birth. Then he is lessly likely to connect his departure from home with the arrival of the baby.

If, on the other hand, your toddler is a born baby-lover the way will be smooth for you. With a minimum of cleverness and co-operation you should avoid the problems of jealousy altogether. Here is a Yorkshire mother's story of her well-deserved success:

'My small daughter was three years old when my baby son was born and it completely changed her little world. She became a mother herself. He was her baby, I was her little girl. She talked, acted and did everything as I did, down to the smallest detail. I had to act the part too and try to be a perfect model of her little girl. Children can make a world of their own at times and almost make adults believe in it too. I thoroughly enjoyed myself, and it got her through a phase which might have been very trying.'

If your toddler is a boy you should not assume he will have a masculine aversion for infants—any more than you should assume a girl will have strong maternal instincts at two or three years old.

At this age many boys are as interested in babies as girls are. I knew a boy of six—the eldest of a family of girls—who was never so happy as surreptitiously borrowing his sisters' dolls. When he went out to tea with other children he always made a bee-line for the dolls' pram or cot.

A Hampshire mother related how her son offered to play a fully maternal role in the care of his new brother. 'One day when feeding my two-month-old baby Timothy, his three-year-old brother Nigel, rolling up his jersey, exclaimed "Mummy, give Timmy a bit of *me*!"'

Many mothers have noticed their toddler imitating his baby brother or sister. Sometimes this is rightly interpreted as a sign of jealousy. But we should not always jump to this conclusion. Several of my toddlers were not in the least jealous of the baby next to them. But they often used to go back to crawling after they had learnt to walk, and loved to crawl about the floor with the baby. They wanted to use the baby's soft hair-brush instead of their own, and even to take a swig at his bottle of orange-juice or boiled water! Did that mean the toddler was jealous? Not at all. It was just a healthy curiosity about something new. Or play-acting. When our toddlers play at 'Mothers and Fathers' we don't immediately assume they are jealous of us. In the same way, playing at being baby need not necessarily mean they are jealous of him. We mustn't get a habit of spotting jealousy where it doesn't exist. The thing to watch is the general behaviour of your toddler, not only one isolated action. If his general behaviour remains normal and happy he is not jealous. But if he is jealous he will almost certainly have become naughty too. Do not worry till that happens.

Casual moments of jealousy are all too human and should not upset us unduly. A Streatham mother's letter illustrates this point. 'I told Andrew, age three-and-a-half, to clear away all his toys as it was bedtime, to which he replied, "My name isn't Andrew; it's Susan," and pointing to his baby sister added "That's Andrew over there!"'

Notice that Andrew was asked to do something all children hate doing—clearing away their toys. He saw baby Susan lying carefree and unconcerned. For her no tiresome duties. A spasm of jealousy shot through him. 'If only I were that lucky baby. Then Mummy wouldn't tell me to put away my toys. She'd do it for me …' Then, with the child's vivid flash from wish to fact, he *was* the baby! But his mother was quite right to smile and not to worry as long as Andrew's general behaviour was normal and happy.

The Older Child is Jealous of the Toddler

Unfortunately jealousy can appear at all stages and ages. A child of six may be just as jealous of a three-year-old as the three-year-old was of the new baby. And often with more reason. For toddlers can be a terrible nuisance.

One of my sons at the age of two was nicknamed 'Destroyer' by his older brothers and sisters. He staggered around destroying their games, scattering soldiers, knocking down bricks. When this sort of thing happens the older children feel it's unfair if Mother protects the toddler from corporal punishment, but does not protect them from his ravages. The next step is for them to say to themselves, 'It's obvious why Mummy's unfair. It's because she loves him more than us . . . ' And at once jealousy—the feeling of not being loved as much as someone else—is rampant.

Personally I usually try to take the side of the older child. No harm is done to the toddler by teaching him to respect other people's things. But a lot may be done to the six-year-old who grows up with a jealous grievance.

It's wonderful how children will help themselves in solving their jealousy problems, provided we parents give them a background of love and security. Writing from Swalecliffe, Kent, a mother describes how her son called in the world of make-believe to help him solve the real problem that faced him.

'When Lawrence was three he would tell us long stories about his imaginary sister, obviously preferring her company to that of his baby brother Patrick. Now that Patrick is three Lawrence has a make-believe friend called Mr Greeder who "hasn't got any little boys", and whose moral support is invaluable in family arguments— "I know it is, Mr Greeder says so!" However, this week Mr Greeder has smashed up his house and gone away.'

There are two points of special note here. First, Lawrence was jealous of Patrick at both stages of his life—as a baby and as a toddler. He invented two different imaginary beings to help him cope with the two different situations. Second, his mother should feel very happy. For the smashing up of Mr Greeder's house symbolised the end of Lawrence's jealousy.

The arrival of a new baby does not often seem to upset a family of several children, though the ex-baby may be jealous for a short time. Of course all children in large families sometimes feel that they might have had more of this world's goods had they not been so many. For instance, my daughters are fond of asking me to give them certain personal belongings of mine they admire 'when you don't want them any more'. I noticed that when a new baby was on the way they always hoped it would be a boy—'or she might want those ear-rings you're going to give me'.

A mother of three small children in Manchester recounts a somewhat similar reaction when she divided equally between them a plate of pie, 'Irene, aged three years, finished hers and asked for another piece. When I explained she had had her share she seemed satisfied. Imagine my surprise when she looked at me sorrowfully and said, "Mummy, why did you have a lot of children?"'

The argument here was clear—a lot of children, a little pie. A few children, lots of pie. However, it would not have been difficult to convince Irene, the youngest, that it was worth while Mummy having three children, and not stopping at the first two!

In general I have never found children really wishing their family were smaller when the question was put to them bluntly. 'Which would you rather? Have enough children in your family to play proper games, act charades and stop you ever feeling lonely, or just be *one*, with a smashing new bike or a doll that stands as high as your waist?' It may be just tact, but they always come down for the large family.

Younger Children are Jealous of Older Ones

This type of jealousy does not seem to be quite so destructive of happiness as the kind described above. Somehow it seems more natural for a younger child to envy his seniors. It is always possible that an element of quite healthy admiration may enter into it. But the jealousy felt by an older child for a younger one is altogether shattering. The elder one feels horribly humiliated as well as being unhappy. It is peculiarly mortifying to envy one's juniors.

A Brentwood mother gives an amusing example of this milder form of the disease. 'Gay, the younger of our two daughters by several years, had two imaginary companions, Tiny Gay and Larling (her own version of "darling"). Apparently to offset her inferior status in the family she would lead them around the house, ostentatiously holding their "hands" about six inches from the floor!' This of course is another instance of an imaginative child using her precious dream-world to solve a very real problem.

Most parents, I suppose, find their younger children at some time or other envying the elder ones' privileges. In our family there are two perennial causes of privilege-jealousy. One concerns the time for going to bed. The other concerns whether or not a child is allowed supper!

Younger children, however, can envy the older ones' sufferings as well as their privileges. A Middlesex mother contributes this anecdote: 'Some years ago my eldest son was inoculated at school against diphtheria. He was showing me his arm and saying how sore it was when the younger one piped up and said he had been inoculated too. I said, "Have you? Show it to me." "I can't," he replied, "I left it at school."'

We've all experienced our toddlers longing to be ill too when another child was laid up in bed. It does no harm to humour them. Take their temperature. Let him share the special diet if it's a nice one.

It is most important that parents should do all they can to prevent their younger children from developing an inferiority complex. I know two sisters the elder of whom is pretty and clever in a conventional way; the younger, more original but less obviously successful. This younger girl was consumed with jealousy. At last she hit on a way of getting even with her sister. If the elder was top of her form, the prettier girl in the school, the most popular . . . well, *she* would be outstanding too, but in the opposite sense. So she went about telling friends and relations she was the ugliest, stupidest most unpopular girl that ever lived. Fortunately her mother spotted this dangerous situation in time. She drew out and emphasised the child's real abilities and ended by having two contented and highly satisfactory daughters.

On the other hand, we parents should not go about hunting for inferiority complexes in our children that may not exist. One conscientious mother realised early on that her younger son was going to turn out considerably less intelligent and less athletic than his elder brother. She felt it her duty to restore the balance. So she set out assiduously to praise and encourage the younger boy, hoping thus to 'even things out' between them. Unfortunately she had only taken into account brains and looks. She had ignored the characters of the brothers. And so it happened that nature had made up to them in differences of temperament any unfairness of mental or physical endowment. The clever elder boy was highly-strung, sensitive and lacking in self-confidence. The fact that his mother never praised him for fear of making the younger one jealous, set up a raging jealousy in the elder one. The younger, as so often happens, combined rather slight mental equipment with a placid and serene temperament. Everyone loved him, while they found his brother 'difficult'. His mother extolled his smallest school successes and implored him not to worry about his failures. And all to no good purpose. For the 'ugly duckling' was no worrier in any case. He did not need special encouragement to make him happy and secure. It was the brilliant son who was the weaker of the two.

The mother had made a mistake. A mistake any of us might make if we tried to practise psychiatry without sufficient investigation and knowledge. The safest rule is to treat all children with absolute fairness and love. Don't hold back a little here or give a little extra there. We are all far too fallible to make these experiments. Give each child all you can.

Children Are Jealous of Outsiders

Nothing is more sacred to a child than his own family circle. Any outsider, even if it is Granny on a long visit, may quite unconsciously cause a jealous outbreak. A mother wrote to me recently: 'My mother is living with us and my young daughter has been very rude to her and seems to resent her presence in the home.' This child, of a sensitive and imaginative nature, already suffered from a sense of insecurity before her Granny came to share her home. This was expressed in acute night fears over a period of several years. When Granny arrived the child evidently felt that she would somehow come between her and her own mother. Unfortunately her father, who might have been able to give his daughter a wider outlet for her affections by sharing the love she reserved entirely for her mother, was not interested in small children, and was waiting for his daughter to reach her teens. An only child, her family circle was altogether too small. It had become in a sense a 'vicious circle', because when an outsider arrived to enlarge it the child's jealous fears urged her to make it smaller. Yet it was originally the very smallness of her family circle that created her insecurity and fears. No wonder her mother noticed with some anxiety that the child 'leans heavily on me'.

The solution was certainly not for the mother to become more aloof, to try to 'make the child stand on her own feet' instead of leaning on her. That would only have made matters worse. She needed to do two things. First, to show by her own undiminished affection that Granny was in no way going to interfere with their relationship. Second, to try if possible to widen the child's affections by bringing about new and stimulating relationships with her Granny and Father.

If the advent of relatives into a small family can upset a child, what of a stranger? No one needs warning at this time of day about the delicate situation created by 'steps', however tactful and well-intentioned. Year by year the pantomime of *Cinderella*, born of the people's own folk-lore, unfolds, however grotesquely, the worst and best than can happen.

A retired schoolmaster from Shropshire recalled the saddest remark made to him during his fifty-one years teaching experience. It was from a seven-year-old boy found crying in the playground. 'I asked what was the matter, and he said, "Please sir, I don't like my mother's husband".' The pathos that smote the schoolmaster so forcibly lay, of course, in the contrast of those last three words. The boy had unconsciously pin-pointed the cold relationship between step-son and stepfather by putting the formal word 'husband' alongside the warmth of 'my mother'. Here, so briefly, was all the old conflict of love and loss, jealousy and loneliness.

Happily most of us can think of examples in our personal experience where a step relationship has healed a wound in the family circle, instead of creating one.

Children Jealous of their Parents

It is not unusual for children of all ages to feel jealous of their father's place in their mother's affections and *vice versa*. Pamela, a four-year-old, had a 'husband'. 'She proudly showed me where he lived—under a stone at the bottom of the garden,' wrote her aunt. 'When I inquired his name I was told "Just Husband".' Yes, that was just it. Pamela had 'my Daddy' but Mummy had 'my husband', and Pamela felt that was somehow better still! Luckily her imagination filled the gap.

Parents of only children must be particularly wary of this kind of jealousy developing. Brothers and sisters protect one another against the impact of their parents' absorption in each other. An only child has no such protection. It feels the full blast of the emotional triangle.

It is quite common for children to express this feeling of being left out by inventing an imaginary friend with the same name as their father. Two stories illustrate this tendency.

'When my daughter was three-and-a-half,' wrote a mother from Wales, 'she was playing one day alone in the garden. I heard her talking to someone. "Who are you talking to?" I asked. "Aggie," she replied. "He went up the tree and has fallen down and is dead." A few days later, again in the garden, I asked her who she was playing with. "Aggie," was again the reply. "Oh, but you said he was dead." "Yes, but he has come to life again." Her father's name was Harry. Hence the Aggie.'

A grandmother from Dover noticed that her four-year-old granddaughter spent a lot of time at the bottom of the garden. 'I asked her what she was doing up there. "Playing with my Bill," came the answer. "But you haven't got a Bill," I said. "Oh yes I have, and he lives in the greenhouse." "But surely you must mean Daddy, as Mummy calls him Bill?" "No, I don't, because this is my 'tend Bill, and he lives in the greenhouse ... " Well, about a year after this the stork brought three little sister triplets, and from then on we heard no more of Bill in the greenhouse.'

Note that in the second story it was the dramatic enlarging of the family circle that put an end to the need for Bill.

I have dealt with a few of the hundred ugly heads which jealousy can rear. They are ugly, of course, in the sense that they cause so much unhappiness if they are allowed to grow and multiply. But the jealousies which spoil the family life are not only found among the children. Parents can become jealous of their own children. This applies specially to the Head of the House. In the last chapters we shall return to some of these things when we come to Father.

17

Fear

'He's absolutely fearless!' I sometimes hear parents say this about their children. It must be lovely to feel so sure. But how often, I wonder, is it strictly true?

One difficulty about our children's fears is that it is not always easy to discover or forestall them. Yet fear is a most disagreeable companion to live with, either as a bed-fellow, or by day. It is the duty of us parents to detect fears, whenever they exist, and then to make every effort to exorcise them.

Here is a letter from Guernsey describing a source of fear familiar to many children, but one which they frequently hide. They feel it would be pooh-poohed if they mentioned it. 'As a child I had a haunting fear which no one ever guessed. Our schoolroom was at the top of the house next to the cistern room, full of alarming water noises. I was convinced that there were water tanks overhead which would one day crash through the ceiling and drown us all. In the evenings the grown-ups and their guests would come up to play noisy games with us. But they never could imagine why the white-faced youngest child always remained rooted to the spot next the door. This was me, and I meant to be the first out when the crash came!'

There is another difficulty in discovering children's fears. It lies in the fact that things which terrify one child may cause delight and amusement to the next. The following story concerns the cistern again, but under what a changed guise! 'My daughter, aged three-and-a-half, has for a year now said that a mouse lives in our airing cupboard. Her name is Missy Mouse and she wears a white dress with red spots and a red sash; she has seven children. When the cistern makes gurgling noises Hazel says, "That's Missy Mouse talking." She knocks on the cistern and asks "Are you at home, Missy Mouse?" and then talks to her.'

Children's fears are as individual as everything else about them. It is impossible to predict with certainty what will or will not frighten any particular child. We must not go about anxiously hunting for fears. But neither must we rule out anything as a possible source of trouble just because most children react favourably towards it. (Father Christmas and Punch-and-Judy are other cases in point.) Once a fear is discovered it must never be laughed at, but always traced to its origins and gently explained away.

Sometimes children's fears are so strange that even the most observant parents would never suspect their existence. We cannot blame ourselves for unwittingly causing these curious fears to arise. But again we can bring them into the open and thus banish them.

Unsuspected Fears

Let us look at some of these queer fears. A mother writes from Southampton saying she tried to give her three-year-old daughter a birthday treat, by having the event announced at Children's Hour on the television programme.

'I told her we must listen at five o'clock, as it would be coming through the loudspeaker. Shortly after we found her in tears and saying, "I don't want to come through the radio!" She seemed to think she had to be folded up and pushed through by the announcer.'

Thomas suffered from another odd fear at an early age. He was afraid no one would ever marry him and he would be alone in the world with no one to care for him after his parents had died. Apparently he infected his sister with this same fear, and Antonia can remember them both lying in bed crying miserably at the thought of their marriageless future! Needless to say no word of this fear was ever breathed to me.

Curiously enough a mother from Ealing seems to have had exactly the opposite trouble with her five-year-old son. 'I discovered Alan sitting up in bed sobbing bitterly because Daddy said he would have to marry when he grew up.' I said this mother *seems* to have had the opposite experience to me. But really the same fear lay at the root of both. It was the fear of losing the love and security of their home. To Alan 'marrying' meant losing his parents, and fending for himself along with a complete stranger.

A third little boy, living at Margate, regarded marriage as the solution to future loneliness, as did my children; but he was more fortunate than they, for he found a 'wife' very early on—in his imagination. 'My son had a slight operation when tiny in a Nursing Home, and realised that babies were born here. So before he left he knocked on the matron's door and ordered a baby girl "to grow up to be my wife". Ever since, until quite recently (he is ten years old now), he has talked of his "wife". He shared his things with her, laughed and talked and played with her.'

Fear of losing their parents is extremely common in children. One of my most dreaded nightmares—a recurring one—was that my mother had shrunk to the size of a tiny doll and died. This fear of loss may show itself in some children by their being abnormally timid and 'tied to mother's apron-strings'.

Others may be unusually possessive with their parents and defiant or rude to strangers.

I remember a small boy of four appearing with both his parents at a children's party. He refused to speak to anyone, and tried to keep his parents penned in with him into a corner of the sofa. If either escaped for a moment to talk to a friend he rushed across the room and dragged them back, like a little sheepdog determined to keep his flock together.

Most parents would naturally be worried and embarrassed by such behaviour. But the only cure is to give *more* love not less. You cannot drive out fear with fear. If you try to 'laugh him out of it' or push him off, you only confirm his worst fears and make him still more clinging. Sending him away from home 'to teach him to stand on his own feet' is to my mind the wrong tactics.

Only when he feels perfectly secure inside his home will he feel safe outside it.

One mother asked me recently what to do about her small son who, with the best intentions and in order to give him a change of scene and more companionship, had been sent a year ago to a holiday home. He had been extremely homesick there and ever since had refused to be parted from his parents for a moment. But holiday time was coming round again. His anxious parents wondered whether they should now make a new effort to dispel his fears by sending him away to a different holiday home, where they hoped conditions would be happier for him.

My advice was on no account to do so. Their son, though merry and gay at home, was still unable to bring himself to speak even to a child he met in the street or out shopping with his mother. I said, 'Where such an unhappy experience has been suffered, it is essential to make the child feel perfectly certain that you never *want* to send him away again. Only when you feel sure he has recaptured his sense of security, can you risk beginning to introduce small doses of "independence". First you might invite a friend to tea with him. If that goes well accept an invitation back to the friend's house—but be sure to go with him yourself, not send him off on his own. Gradually, he will venture out with confidence into the world beyond his own doorstep.'

Fathers are occasionally an obstacle to what they regard as this 'soft' treatment. They are afraid of increasing the child's timidity by pandering to it. I am afraid they sometimes feel their own vanity is injured by not having a 'manly' son, and they hope there is a quick way out of the trouble. But these troubles connected with deep-rooted fears can never be exorcised quickly. Mothers, who spend more time with the child and know his anxieties better, should stand firm on this point.

Childish and Adult Fears

It is not only the strangeness of children's fears and the fact that they are frequently hidden from us that makes it difficult for parents to detect them. There is another reason why we are so often wide of the mark in our interpretations of their emotions. This is the adults' tendency to judge children by their own reactions. Because a certain child is not frightened of things that frighten us, we blithely assume he is frightened of nothing at all. 'He's absolutely fearless.'

On the whole I should say that children's fears seldom coincide with those of adults. Take war, for instance. A London mother tells how she needlessly tried to protect her two-year-old daughter from a fear she never felt. 'During an air-raid I got my little daughter out of bed. I suppose she sensed that I was nervous, for she said, "Don't be frightened, Mummy; I won't let anyone hurt you".' Here the roles were reversed, the child detecting the adult's fears and trying to banish them.

Children are often recklessly bold about material dangers which horrify their elders. Jumping traffic, climbing cliffs or trees, being driven excessively fast in cars—few of these things make them turn a hair. I well remember being driven by taxi in a dense fog up in Yorkshire. Thomas and Patrick were absorbed in telling me the plot of a film, but I was too nervous to listen and made all the wrong comments. The taximan seemed to be going at a breakneck speed. At last he realised my anxiety, and turning round, said in his kindly Yorkshire voice: 'It's all right, Muther, Ah'll get you there.' The boys roared with laughter and quoted it against me for years.

It is extraordinary how frequently grown-ups expect children to be frightened of large animals and how seldom they are. When they are, it is too often because grown-ups have infected them with their own fears. Here is a Sheffield father who remembers his first intro-duction to the quietest of domestic animals—the cow. 'My mother took me to pick blackberries. We were on a hill, and suddenly a lot of cows came running towards us. My mother was terrified of cows. She grabbed me and dragged me down the hill screaming all the way. The cows had come down for a drink of water!'

Another father, this time from Llanelli, tells how a man tried to reassure a small boy who was not in the least alarmed. 'When my son was but two-and-a-half, I took him round a market garden. A large bull-terrier came towards us, but I knew he would not be afraid.

One of the men, however, came up to him and said: "It's all right, it won't hurt you, it's only a pig." My son laughed and replied, "And you are a big donkey!" What a laugh we all had.'

No, we must turn away from the newspaper world of accidents and sudden death, mad bulls and savage hounds, to a world far more vague and intangible, if we are to lay bare the sources of our children's fears.

With my own children, I found that it was the slightly mysterious, inexplicable things, which were most likely to disturb them. The fly which suddenly alights from nowhere on one's pram cover—this used to terrify Antonia to such an extent that I had to put a mosquito net over her during the summer.

Judith, when she had long out-grown the pram stage, could not bear the sound of a daddy-long-legs drumming his legs together in her bedroom at night. Even though Rachel shared her room and was quite unconcerned—indeed, no one else in the family had taught her to be afraid of insects or suggested they were anything but curious and amusing—still Judith felt an uncontrollable horror. The only thing I found that did a little good was to catch a daddy-long-legs and show it to her under a magnifying-glass. She could not help being intrigued by the delicate drum-sticks with tiny knobs on the end.

I have found in fact that a magnifying-glass is a faithful friend in helping to dispel the smaller concrete fears which children suffer from. Horror of slugs and worms is quite understandable, but a close-up view of almost any animal, insect or plant completely transforms it in the child's imagination. Perhaps the child who is the subject of the following poignant tale had been successfully trying out this method: 'My small son came in from the garden crying because he had killed a slug. I told him he had killed lots of slugs and snails before, so why cry over this one? He replied, "Well, Mummy, this was only a baby and it was fast asleep: the others were all grown-ups and they could see me coming".'

Some children seem very susceptible to the vibrations attendant on loud noises. Rachel once said it was the shaking of thunder she did not like. Thomas, when still under two years old, was passionately fond of trains. One day I took him to Aylesbury station to see a real train for the first time. As I held him up in my arms and the great giant roared into view, Thomas began to tremble violently. I felt I could hardly hold him, but when the train had passed the trembling subsided. Thinking I had made a terrible mistake and nearly frightened him to death, I hastened towards the exit. But a yell of disappointment and arms outstretched towards the platform made me realise that his love for the train was even greater than his fear of its awe-inspiring presence.

Thunder, low-flying planes and trains seem to batter them physically with their din and vibration, but mentally they are an intoxicating pleasure.

To sum up. Children's fears, like all fears, may cause much damage and misery unless they are discovered and allayed by sympathetic parents. Even a fear which seems to you incredibly foolish must be taken seriously. Do not try to 'laugh away' children's fears. It is better to explain them away by getting to the bottom of them. But try as we will, we cannot always banish completely the deep irrational fears which disturb them.

Prominent among the most baffling of these fears, because partly primitive in origin, are those that beset children when night falls.

18

Afraid of the Dark

'From ghosties and ghoulies and long-legged beasties, and all things that go bump in the night, good Lord deliver us . . . ' So said grown-up people in the Middle Ages. No wonder our children still have night fears!

Being afraid of the dark is so common in children that most of us do not worry about it unduly. In my family, only Thomas, Michael and Kevin have never *shown* any fear of the dark (though even they may have felt it but succeeded in concealing their feelings). Some children, however, seem to have an over-dose of this atavistic feeling. They suffer from real night terrors; and if no cure can be found by their parents, may have to be taken to visit an experienced psychiatrist in a child guidance clinic.

These children will not go to sleep without a light in their room and someone sitting by them to keep them company. Or after a few hours sleep they wake up with a nightmare, for they have fallen asleep buried under the bedclothes and are feeling suffocated. It is a matter of moments before they are screaming for Mummy or Daddy, and the whole wearying paraphernalia of 'getting them off to sleep' has to be gone through again.

Such unfortunate children can be a misery to themselves and a problem to their parents. Most parents feel that they can cope with almost anything during the day, provided there is peace at night. That longing for the peace that falls when all the children are at last in bed and asleep becomes almost obsessional if one is continually deprived of it. It is harder to be patient with a child who will not, or cannot, get to sleep, than any other. And yet it is more important than ever to be gentle and kind. Some fathers have a special gift for soothing their sleepless child. Others add to the mother's difficulties by wearily urging their wife to 'let them cry it out'.

One mother wrote to me in despair over a situation of this kind. 'J. is nearly seven years old, and an only child. Up to the age of four-and-a-half she was placid and happy. Then we moved into a larger house and from that time she developed fears of being alone at night. I tried various ways of consoling her but nothing would satisfy her but my presence. . . . Matters gradually improved, until she saw a pantomime, and this started it all over again. However, I managed to keep her away from entertainments of this sort until by chance recently she was allowed to see a television serial at a friend's house. . . . I just feel that I must know if I am coping properly with her. I sit with her until she goes to sleep, but after a few hours she wakens during the night crying. I have allowed her to come into my room, but this is happening every night, and I am wondering whether she is taking advantage of the situation. . . . My husband does not agree with my method, and says that I am spoiling the child, and that she should be made to face up to it.'

I must say at once that I advised this mother to take her child to a child guidance clinic unless the trouble subsided pretty rapidly. There is a good deal of difference between a child who wakes up in the night continually, and one who makes a fuss about going to sleep. The first cannot possibly be waking herself up on purpose, and therefore cannot be 'taking advantage' of soft treatment. In the second case there may be some element of wilful refusal to settle off to sleep, which of course is much easier to deal with.

I have quoted this letter fairly fully because I feel it may be of help to other parents who have had the same trying experiences. It is clear, for instance, that some outside event in J.'s life has come to upset her previously happy existence. There are several possibilities to choose from. The new, larger house. Her relations with her father and mother; and possibly other relatives. I should be surprised to learn that the pantomime on television had done more than recall, in some way, a fear that was already in the child's mind. I might add that this wise mother was only too glad to seek the understanding advice of a trained psychiatrist.

In my own experience, continual waking up in the night is nearly always due to some loss or unhappiness the child has sustained in her waking hours. One of my daughters, at the age of seven, caused me considerable anxiety by suddenly starting a cycle of this kind. Like most mothers, I began by trying to cure it with various small physical devices. First she was given a bedside light of her own (she slept with two other children and added to the chaos by waking them up as well as me), and told to switch it on and read a book until she fell asleep again. This did no good. Human companionship was what she wanted. 'Why should everyone else in the house be asleep and only me awake?' she protested tearfully.

Then I tried giving her a box of biscuits to nibble at when she woke up in case it was due to some form of 'night starvation'. This was no good either. The biscuits gave her indigestion and the other children soon discovered her secret hoard and helped her gobble them up. At last I called in the doctor, who gave a mild sedative to be taken at bedtime. But in his wisdom he made it clear that he thought the trouble was probably psychological, and might require special treatment if continued.

The medicine seemed to work at first. But unfortunately it tasted so nasty that she had to drink tumblers and tumblers of water to take the taste away. This was enough in itself to make sure of waking her up in the middle of the night as before. However, I then settled down seriously to consider what could be the root cause of the trouble. I decided it was mainly the loss of a very dear old friend who had been a kind of fairy godmother to her. This friend had suddenly fallen ill, and was now only rarely seen.

So I started on a new tack. The child was given special attention and extra affection to make up for the love she had lost. At the same time I said to her: 'If you can get through the night without waking up, you can have a penny in the morning. It doesn't matter if you wake up for a few minutes, as long as you shut your eyes again quickly and go off to sleep without waking anyone else. You will be given your penny just the same. If you can get through a whole week, what a lovely collection of pennies you will have.'

I am glad to say that within a fortnight this double approach of extra attention by day, and a small bribe at night to make the child's own effort of will seem worth while, had borne fruit. The first few nights she admitted to having still wakened in the small hours and stayed awake for a quarter of an hour or so. 'But I shut my eyes tight, like you said, and went off to sleep again.' I gave her a penny each morning and congratulated her on her achievement. At the end of two weeks she was sleeping through the night, and the penny-giving had been tacitly stopped.

When I told our doctor he was delighted, and pointed out that it must have meant a certain amount of will-power on her part to get over the first few nights, and break the habit of waking. When I asked dubiously what I should do if it all started up again, he said with a glint, 'You can offer her 2d!'

Some Causes and Cures

Now I want to turn to some of the other things which I know from experience have frightened children at night, and give brief accounts of how I have tried to cope with them.

DARKNESS—Children spend the bright day in company. When darkness falls and they feel extra need of companionship they are often shut up alone in bed. Such are the contradictions of civilisation! I find the best solution is to switch off the bedroom light, but leave the door open and the light on in the passage. One of my daughters, however (the one who later began to suffer from insomnia), used to plead, 'Please leave the door open and the light on in my room.' I always readily agreed, despite the danger of 'forming bad habits'. It was obvious that she had already formed a regrettable habit—fear of the dark. Going to sleep peacefully with a light on was a less bad habit than crying in the darkness. Of course I switched both lights off when she was asleep.

LONELINESS—This, together with darkness and silence which combine to heighten the sense of isolation, I believe to be the chief cause of simple or 'normal' night fears. A letter from Camforth, Lancs., expresses with poignancy and logic an only child's feelings of loneliness at night. 'My four-year-old daughter woke up in the middle of the night and when I came to her said, "Why do mummies and daddies sleep in the same room together and leave little girls to sleep by themselves?"'

There are several ways in which we can help. Nervous children are comforted by sharing a room with a brother or sister. All my children have had to share a bedroom with one or two brothers or sisters. They have certainly appreciated this arrangement and never clamoured for 'a room of my own' until the teens were reached. Shared bedrooms bring disadvantages of their own—noise, and different age-groups keeping each other awake at night and wakening each other too early in the morning. But they do banish that awful feeling of isolation in most cases.

For the only child, we must try to find some other 'companion'. Anything *alive* will often fill the bill, if the child is not too young. A pet dog or cat sleeping in the same bedroom has been known to work wonders. Nor do I think it is unhygienic or in any other way to be deprecated.

But it would not be wise to leave an animal with a very small child. Fortunately toddlers have their own effective methods of dealing with this problem. Teddies and cuddly toys will act as comforters—live ones—and prevent them feeling cut off from the world.

From Cornwall comes the story of a stuffed toy which was very much alive and provided as much fun and companionship as any real brother or sister. 'My small daughter was tucked up for the night. I was sitting having a quiet read when I heard shouts and laughter coming from upstairs. When I went up to see what it was all about she informed me: "Teddy is kicking me out of bed!" This went on for some time till I had to "spank" Teddy and tell him to behave and go to sleep. After that all was quiet.'

Another somewhat older girl from Watford consciously uses her toy family to take the place of a human one, and at the same time to help her bridge the gulf between waking and sleeping. 'My seven-year-old daughter invests her large toy monkey with the authority of a father over all her dolls and stuffed animals, with herself as mother. She tells me that every night after I have put her to bed they all go off to Dollies' Land, returning at ten minutes to six each morning, which is the exact time the alarm clock rouses me and I peep into her bedroom.'

Both these stories and many others which every parent could add to the list, show how important play and toys are in the child's life. Toys, and an imagination unfettered by adult criticism or ridicule, can help both parents and children over many difficulties, large and small.

Not that even toys are essential. The wonderful imagination of children can do its work, if necessary, unaided. Sometimes it seems to prefer to work in the void. Here are three anecdotes, not unalike, showing how children, when allowed to give free rein to their imagination, can create companions out of thin air. How invaluable such companions are at bedtime! 'When Christopher was aged three years he had two make-believe friends called Chevron and Denton. They were his constant companions. He would lie perched on the edge of his bed, "'Cos Chevron and Denton have crept into my bed tonight, Mummy".'

Wendy, also aged three, was found by her mother shivering on the edge of the bed. 'Hush!' she whispered, 'Lucket's just asleep.' (Lucket was her inseparable, imaginary friend.) 'Don't wake her, but she's got all the bed and all the blankets too!' Wendy was quite ready to sacrifice mere physical comfort for the sake of a companion to conquer the loneliness of bedtime.

This third story concerns a child who was definitely cured of night fears by the remedial use of her imagination. She is a mother herself now, and this is how she remembers the nights of fear and the way she overcame them: 'Being an only child I loved to mix with children of large families. But bedtime was a nightmare. I lay awake beneath the sheets, head bathed in sweat, afraid of I knew not what. So always I loved to pretend I lived with the Bruin boys of *The Rainbow*. Often I had seen them sharing one huge bed. My place was in the middle with the various animals on other side. I grew so bold that I would sit up in the dark, surrounded by my friends, and dare the powers of darkness to do their worst.'

There is one simple way in which a mother can directly help to remove the child's feeling of isolation and of being cut off from the world in his lonely tower. This is by staying upstairs for a little while after you have tucked up your child and said good night to him. You can move about doing odd jobs so that he can hear your quiet and comforting footsteps. He may even fall asleep before he hears his mother's footsteps receding downstairs. I myself can still hear, in memory, the sinister and final shutting of the door downstairs, if, on some occasion, my mother had to go down before I had fallen asleep. But more often the sounds from the outside world gradually mingled together in a soothing monotone and I was asleep before the fatal door shut. It is well worth dawdling around a bit upstairs to give our children the chance to avoid that particular pang.

Children who go to Sunday school or have some other religious training are in a strong position when night falls. One small girl assured her mother that Jesus was watching over her; she could see his eyebrow—the crescent moon!

Personally I strongly deprecate the view that religious training actually increases a child's night fears, by making him 'superstitious'. It is no doubt true that the supernatural, if handled in the wrong way, can contribute to nervous apprehensions already in the child. But in my opinion children's 'numinous' (religious or supernatural) sense is inborn, and a religious training will channel these instincts, which in any case would exist in the child, into the right direction. My own experience is that a belief in the loving protection of God, at night as at all other times, is the child's greatest defence of all against nameless fears. It grows in power and efficacy as the child's understanding deepens.

THE MOON—Kevin, my youngest, loved the moon and was always held up to say 'Good night' to it. In fact, the moon was to him a goddess who, when she shone, gave him a powerful motive for going to bed. 'I want to go up and see the moon.'

But other mothers have found that the moon inspired their children with fear, especially in strange propensity to wax and wane and then disappear altogether.

'The moon is b-broken,' sobbed one child, and another, on being told it was not broken, insisted, 'Well, it's torn then.' A third exclaimed, 'Someone has bitten a piece out of the moon—who did it?' I knew a ten-year-old who was herself 'moon bitten'. She was always sick if she slept in its light.

There are two remedies. One is to give the child an interesting account of what the moon really is, and how it works. This is the method I favour. The other is to keep the bedroom curtains drawn, even at the risk of excluding a little of that pearl beyond price—fresh air.

BEDROOM SURROUNDINGS—Curtains moving silently in the breeze are always eerie. If your child is of a nervous disposition it is better to hang curtains made of a fairly heavy material and lined, which will not flutter about so much as the lighter stuff.

Valances round beds can be another source of disquiet. I made some for Judith and Rachel when we moved house. They looked charming but definitely started up a new train of night fears. In the tradition of our great-grandmothers, they began to imagine someone was lurking underneath and took flying leaps into bed. Shadows, reflections in mirrors, the strange shapes of furniture and ornaments in the half-light, are all common causes of fear. For this reason I am inclined to favour the rather plain and austere fashions in internal decoration of children's bedrooms which reigned ubiquitously in the 'thirties'. Buttons and bows, flounces and frills on bed and dressing-table are better avoided with nervous children.

Lastly there are all the noises of the night—creaking boards, rattling windows, the sound of the wind. Robert Louis Stevenson's famous poem, *Windy Nights*, was to me, as a child, the very epitome of midnight weirdness and terror.

> Whenever the moon and the stars are set,
> Whenever the wind is high,
> All night long in the dark and wet,
> A man goes riding by.

I used to recite these words with a mixture of delight and dread.

When Thomas was two years old he woke up during a high wind and called out, 'Take Thomas into Mummy's bed! Wind blow Thomas out of window.' I took him into bed, defying what were then 'modern' rules. (I think the mothers of today are less rule-bound than we were. When we broke 'the rules' it was with a sense of guilt. I have not noticed it with this new generation of young mothers. They realise that the textbooks are made for the child, and not the child for the textbooks.) At any rate, I took Thomas into bed with me. For the first rule of all is to drive out fear, whichever way you choose to do it.

19

Bedtime

Sometimes one is tempted to feel that children are not really so different from grown-ups after all. But when it comes to bedtime there is a difference big enough to impress all of us. I feel about my bed as a caterpillar must feel about his chrysalis a few days before he's due to 'turn in'. Samuel Pepys ended each day of his diary with a contented sigh—'And so to bed.' But we have to end our children's day too often with a thundered roar—'And GO to bed!'

So I was not surprised when the light evenings brought letters about bedtime, including this one from a West London family. 'What about some hints on children's bedtime? It's a subject my husband and I often discuss.' (I quote this sentence because of its reference to Father, who has a special interest in his children having a peaceful and uninterrupted bedtime!)

To begin with, there are luckily many children who are as chrysalis-minded as any grown-up. No need to drive them up to bed. My youngest son, Kevin, is one of these. He often suggests bed himself, before his scheduled time, and we drift upstairs as placidly as one of those idealised pictures in a 'Bedtime Story'.

But on the whole I think the anti-bed type of child is more usual. Antonia and Thomas, when young, were inveterate bed-haters. I found it most distressing to end every day, however successful it had been up till then, with a long wrangle over bedtime. At last, one evening, I decided this must stop. A new tactic was called for. There should be no more struggles. Bedtime, tonight, should be settled by them. So I said, 'All right, then. Don't go to bed if you don't want to. Sit up as long as you please.' I added, as if as an afterthought, 'Of course you know that I always have work to do in the evening, so I shall not be able to read to you or talk. And you will have to put yourselves to bed when you do decide to go.'

It worked beautifully. They sat up, on principle, till 10 p.m., their usual bedtime being six o'clock. But next evening there was no mention of another vigil.

Why do children object to bedtime? When I put this question to Judith, who is now getting on for fourteen, and is reminded of bedtime but never ordered off, she said: 'It is really the awful feeling of being shut away up there.' That made me think that in very cold countries the mothers must have one problem less; for there all the family sleep on or around the stove. There is no 'shutting away'.

This answer really brings us back again to the night fears, which have already been discussed. Undoubtedly these fears are responsible for the extreme unwillingness of imaginative children to go to bed. And children are an imaginative race. So we must always be ready to give a prominent place to this all-pervading source of trouble.

But I believe there is another, simpler cause of the very general dislike of bedtime. It is just that 'downstairs' is more fun than 'upstairs'. Why go to bed, where everything comes to an end, when you could still be in the warm bright room with Daddy and Mummy and the rest of the family, where life still goes on? It is such a natural feeling. And there is usually such an easy way round it, without that six o'clock scene.

In one sentence, make 'upstairs' as attractive as 'downstairs'. To start with, try to avoid a sudden break between playtime and bedtime. Let bedtime also be a playtime, in its own way. Merge the two together. Never find yourself suddenly making an abrupt announcement, such as 'Past six already! Quick! Put all your things away. Off to bed at once!'

If you are to achieve a smooth transition you must keep your eye on the clock. Fire off warnings, like minute guns (only very gentle ones!). 'I shouldn't get out another puzzle now. It's nearly six. . . . Five minutes more, then up we go. . . . I'm going to race you to the door in two minutes . . . '

After due warning the flag drops. We're off!

I will divide the journey into three stages. Stairs. Bath. Bed.

The first hurdle is obviously to get them out of the playroom and up the stairs on to the top landing. Often this hurdle is quite the worst—a real Beecher's Brook—and the rest is comparatively easy going.

I find it a good thing, unlike jockeys I believe, to 'rush' the stairs. If you allow your child to dawdle or drag up them, you start bedtime off on the wrong foot. It is possible to get *into* bed on the wrong side, as well as out of it. So make it a race upstairs, or a pick-a-back. Be a horse and let them drive *you* up instead of you driving them. Be a queen leading a procession. Be a Wat Tyler leading a revolution. Be anything. But not a mother dragging Shakespeare's boy 'like snail unwillingly to'—bed. Bismarck once said, 'You can do anything with children if you play with them.' He would have been a great statesman in the home.

A Dublin mother was presented with a perfect way of getting up the stairs and into the bathroom. 'My son was a seal. He had to go upstairs on flippers and tail. Bathtime was a perpetual fishing for imaginary herrings. Washing had to be managed in between.' That, in my opinion, is the secret of the bathtub. Washing and drying should always be done 'in between'. Most children dislike it. Either you get the soap into their eyes or up their nose; or you accidentally rub 'my graze' (it is extraordinary what sinister importance even the most microscopic scratch achieves in the bath!) or you just rub too hard. One small girl protested to her mother while being dried, 'Don't scrub me so hard or you'll rub all the white off!'

Games in the bath can rival games in the playroom. So try not to worry about a few splashes if you want bedtime to be a popular event. A wet bath-sheet and a flowing sea on the lino are a small price to pay for six o'clock smiles.

You may find your child has some secret fear of the bathroom which puts him off bedtime. Don't try to hustle such a fear away just because it's so absurd and you are in a hurry. When the stage of vivid imagination is passed, the fear will pass too, leaving no traces. You need not feel that by 'pandering' to it you will be encouraging neurotic tendencies in your child. Treat it as this mother did from Billericay. 'My son had an imaginary little man who lived in the bathroom. Until I took the man by the hand and led him out my boy would refuse to undress and have his bath.'

The gurgling of the waste-pipe is a common cause of fear. Never try to get your child out of the bath by threatening. 'If you don't hurry I'll pull out the plug and send you down.' You may set up a whole train of neuroses. On the other hand, as we saw in an earlier chapter, the same sound which is frightening to one child may be intriguing to others. I have heard of several instances of children who believe a 'friend' lives at the bottom of the waste-pipe and each evening they listen eagerly to hear him 'talking'.

An inexpensive visit to the shops can help to make the evening bath something to look forward to—to run up for. Try a 'children's edition' of everything they use in the bathroom. Soap made like a rabbit or bear; a sunset towel (this is the name given to her red and orange towel by Catherine); a tooth-brush with Mickey Mouse or some other sprite upon it; and toothpaste flavoured like your fruit garden.

The Last Stage

Now for the last stage—bed. Begin by making the room into a place the child will like to be in for its own sake. James Barrie wrote a play about 'the island that likes to be visited'. Make hers a bedroom she likes to visit. Everybody knows about children's special curtain materials and wall-paper. But now there are new low-watt light bulbs, whose filaments form a glowing picture of the Man in the Moon or some other figure to make the night seem enchanting.

Let your child cover the walls with her own pictures; big vivid sheets painted, perhaps, at school. Children love to run upstairs to take another peep at their works of art. Besides, their own paintings can never be frightening.

It is surprising how even the most innocent adult picture, hung on a child's bedroom wall, may be misunderstood and interpreted as some weird horror. I remember an engraving that adorned my bedroom as a child. It showed a shepherd and shepherdess running hand-in-hand through a meadow—a harmless enough subject in all conscience. The shepherd's cloak billowed out gaily behind them as they ran. But from my bed the fatal cloak made the whole picture look to me like a huge skull.

The next question, and almost the last, is how to get your child *into* bed, willingly and happily. It is here that fantasy and make-believe, the mother's faithful handmaids, make their own valuable contribution.

When Kevin was about four I found he would always jump quickly into bed if I suggested he was a rabbit hopping into his hole. This method was so successful that I passed it on to other mothers, and do so here. But I must admit there was one failure. A mother sent in her 'progress report' after trying out the new plan: 'I told my son to be a good little bunny and show me how he could hop into his hole. He did so. Five minutes later I heard a voice, "Look, Mummy, how the little bunny can hop out again!"'

Perhaps it is better to turn the rabbit into a guinea-pig for specially active children, as one parent did. She wrote: 'I quite agree that a game of "let's be something or other" can change almost any awkward mood. And for soothing and quieting at bedtime, "you be a baby guinea-pig and I am its mummy putting it into its little nest" always seems to work.' Guinea-pigs have short legs and stay put!

The last point about bedtime is a fairly obvious one, recognised I am sure by all parents; but not always by well-meaning friends and visitors, who are fond of working the children up to a frenzy of excitement with a bedtime romp. In fact bedtime should not end on a boisterous note. Let the tempo decline gently, like the end of a Greek play. Try to have a peaceful, familiar ritual, with an 'epilogue' the child knows and likes and can see coming from afar.

I suggest a very short story read aloud by you on the child's bedside; prayers; and your final kiss. As for your last words—every parent has his own 'good night'.

As a tail-piece to this chapter I cannot resist including a letter which reached me from a Cheshire mother, Mrs Gertrude Moffat. It puts, as well as possible, the point of view of the successful parent who feels she can get along all right without any 'tips', 'hints', 'dodges', 'points' or gadgetty advice on upbringing from experts or otherwise.

It is a good thing for writers and 'experts' to keep a sense of proportion. To remember, in the midst of giving advice and receiving requests for help, that there are thousands of mothers who find the light of nature a perfectly adequate guide. Thank goodness there are! It is a light that sometimes fails. And when it does, the rest of us can perhaps shed a beam on dark places. But in our zeal to help the ones in difficulties we may inadvertently give the impression that parenthood is an infinitely complicated job requiring immense sublety, ingenuity and cleverness to make it work at all. Of course this is not true; and the following letter puts all of us 'tipsters' in our right place.

'What is all this poppycock about putting children to bed? Honestly, I've never had to be a mummy guinea-pig, or hop up the stairs on all fours, and as for sunset towels . . .

'What a prosaic household ours must be. Tonight, as my children, aged three, five and seven, step out of the bath (ordinary colour and shape) and I dry them on a plain white towel, and as they later lie contented and happy in their beds with nothing more frivolous than a Mickey Mouse cartoon to divert their worldly little eyes, I shall be thinking with amusement of all these fantastic folk in their Wonderland of bunnies and hedgehogs!'

20

A Teenager in the Home

I had better say at once that I intend to concentrate as far as possible on the fifteens and under. Are the over-fifteens still *children* in the sense that the word has been used for centuries?—immature beings distinct from adults to whom they owe obedience, in return for which they get the benefit of an 'upbringing'. Indeed it is by no means certain today that fourteen-year-olds are children any longer. Are there such things as children in the old sense?

Not long ago the portrait of a ravishing 'child' of fourteen graced the cover of a magazine. It was a poignant study in contrasts: the poise, the sophisticated hairpieces and the provocative see-through dress of an adult, contradicting the fawnlike fragility and sensitive dreaminess of a child—a child who seemed already to feel nostalgia for a youth that was going to pass away almost before it had arrived. Of course she was still at school, but the caption proclaimed:

'GIRL OF OUR TIME—*a girl without a childhood*' adding that this was 'twentieth century progress'.

Even the least imaginative parent must see that if these are the Girls of Our Time, they and we are in for some surprises.

For one thing, we may be using all the wrong words. Ten years ago the name 'teenager' was quite acceptable, almost complimentary. Today it appears less and less often. It seems to smack of ankle-socks. But what collective alternatives can you find? Young people— youth—adolescents—none of those names is perfect.

The truth is that in order to establish a relationship with what used to be called teenagers, you must try to forget age altogether. Don't think of yourself as old and them as young. Think in terms of people, individuals. The whole antiquated confrontation of age and youth bores them. We must try to sweep it away. Then they may listen to us, just as we ourselves are ready to listen to people we respect, no matter what their age. Interest in the subject of age is one of the great divides between little children and young adults. The opening remark of a small child to another he meets for the first time is 'How old are you?' followed by 'What's your name?' By twenty-one that kind of labelling seems to take a back place. My youngest daughter often comes home from a party having met someone new she can describe vividly; but when I ask their name and age she hasn't the slightest idea. So I too will move away from precise ages. I will think of boys and girls who are living at home, are still attending school, and have not yet started work. When they first went to school the great interest was fitting them into the new environment of school. Now the challenge is fitting them into the home.

Have you ever noticed a contradiction in children as they grow up? When they are small they love to help in the home. But what happens when they reach a stage when they could be really useful? Mother begs for help—but answer comes there none. Of if there is an answer, it's a grumpy one: 'Oh, do leave me alone, Mummy … stop nagging … I'm busy …'

A mother writes to me for advice about her two teenage daughters. 'They used to be good home-loving girls, but now they stand and argue with me if I insist on them helping me. They won't wash a stitch of their clothes without a scene. What have I done, or where have I gone wrong? I've always gone without to let them have the best I can.'

What a sad state of affairs. A father, who has also written to me on this subject, comments bitterly, 'When anything goes wrong the parents are always to blame.'

How can disillusioned parents begin to remedy this family impasse? We must try to look at our teenagers with fresh eyes and study them with a mixture of love and shrewdness. To begin with, they are facing at least four different, awkward relationships. 1. With themselves. 2. With their parents. 3. With their brothers and sisters. 4. With the outside world. Without taking sides it may be possible to analyse some of these relationships in a helpful way.

Teenagers are at Loggerheads with Themselves

Teenage might equally well be called 'between-age'. Every teenager is painfully aware of being at a half-way house. Half-way between a child and an adult. It's an uncomfortable feeling. They feel they get the worst of both worlds—while wanting the best. Antonia remembers it clearly: the urge to keep all the irresponsibility of a child, and win all the privileges of an adult. No housework and lots of late nights.

At the same time they are desperately coping with the physical changes that occur in themselves. They suddenly become self-conscious and shy. A fatal new facility for blushing is discovered. It happens whenever they speak or are spoken to by anyone outside the immediate family circle. The only solution seems to be a vow of perpetual silence and solitude, or a mad torrent of words to distract attention from the red cheeks.

Plumpness spells acute misery. Never make your daughter go on wearing clothes that have got a little too tight. There is no shame like the shame of bursting seems and strained zips, or even allegedly self-supporting stockings that won't stay up because the thighs are the wrong shape. You must lay out the necessary sum on tights.

Boys make queer noises when they speak. My son Patrick's voice broke while he was away at school. He arrived home all agog for the holidays. His younger brothers and sisters were equally excited over his return. But when the hero opened his mouth to speak there was a spontaneous outburst of incredulous laughter. I shall never forget Patrick's expression of mingled pride and embarrassment at this unrehearsed tribute to his new powers.

On the whole I think parents fail in sympathy towards teenage troubles more often than they do towards the troubles of other stages of childhood. Phrases such as 'fancy doing such a thing at your age—a great girl like you' leap to our lips and cause deep hurts. We forget that the girl or boy who is big in size is still very small in self-confidence and ease. It is particularly hard for us parents to remember that a child's problems do not grow progressively lighter as he grows older.

The truth is that the 'difficult years' occur in irregular patches all through childhood. Seven to nine are usually far more difficult years than three to five. Four is often a perfect age; the adjustments from babyhood have been achieved, but the imagination is still in full play, undeterred by the hard realities that will so soon follow. In the same way twelve to fourteen is a more difficult period for the child to cope with than, say, nine to twelve. Yet just because the fourteen-year-old may be a 'great girl' and the ten-year-old is still a little one, we expect more from the older child and give less. A ten-year-old who cuts his knee gets far more sympathy than a teenager who feels moody. Yet the plight of the second is more to be pitied.

It may be that nature herself is partly responsible. No doubt the maternal instinct of protectiveness does diminish as a child achieves greater and greater physical strength. But that is no reason why other maternal functions based on love, sympathy and understanding, should diminish too. In fact, these *conscious* parental activities ought to increase during the child's teens.

How many mothers take their older children's troubles as seriously as the same child's teething troubles years ago? The mother who sat up all night with a fractious baby will not sit up half an hour when that baby has become a teenage daughter out at a party. The fact that the girl herself may want nothing less than an exhausted but still vigilant parent sitting up for her, seems somehow to let the parent off. By an unspoken mutual agreement both sides slip out of their responsibilities. And the crucial question of what time a school-girl ought to be in bed is discussed too late, in an atmosphere of bad temper caused by long days and short nights. Or the troublesome schoolchild may be a boy. When he was a baby and seemed fretful his mother was only too eager to make excuses for him: 'Poor little fellow, he must have wind.' But now he has grown into a teenager, subject to sulks, struggling with corn-crake voice, incipient beard, spots and blushes, he gets short shrift. 'I can't think *why* he's like this. . . . He used to be so easy.'

Teenagers make themselves quite as unhappy as they make their parents. It is our job to reconcile them to themselves. This is rarely achieved by direct criticism. For the typical teenager is already self-critical to an excessive degree. No, the right medium is always love, based on real interest and knowledge.

Your daughter feels she is a lump, a drudge, an overgrown child, an immature adult? Yet in her secret heart nothing will ever convince her—and rightly so—that she is not a fairy princess. It is in your power to help her translate this dream into an even more enthralling reality.

Operation Parents

We have seen that teenage is in some sense a battlefield. Just because the teenager is so often at war with himself he finds it hard to get on with the rest of the family. A particular state of tension seems to exist between him and his parents. Fundamentally it appears to rest on a natural feeling of rivalry between the young 'stag' and the old 'stag', the young 'queen' and the old 'queen bee'. There is nothing wrong in this. But whereas in nature the young move off as soon as this state of rivalry looks like developing, in the human family the two generations must go on living under the same roof for at least a year or two.

How can we of the older generation help our teenagers to conduct their campaigns with the minimum of losses on both sides? To live under a common roof that is more like a roof-tree than a prison ceiling?

A correspondent from Edinburgh gives the answer in simple words: 'I do wish parents would try to remember what they were like when young, and then they would understand their own children.' Parents must indeed be like Peter Pan—and never quite grow up. Before you ask your teenager to tidy her room (a thing you mustn't fail to do) take a look—in retrospect—at your own bedroom twenty years ago. I can remember my mother surveying the incredible chaos in my drawers and saying blankly, 'I give you up.' Yet today I am almost painfully tidy. Teenage really is a time on its own, and gives only the barest hint of the final product. There is no need to despair.

'Come and Give Me a Hand'

One of the commonest causes of strife is in fact the mother's demand for her daughter's help in the home. Every mother is perfectly right to make this demand—of boys as well as girls. If she does all the chores herself 'for the sake of peace and quiet' she is not training her children properly.

But it is wise to make the order addressed to the ten-year-old into a polite request to the teenager. And even in the sacred cause of 'good training' it is not worth having a scene or show-down. For nothing is so important at this stage as affectionate relations between the parent and teenager. Anything which really jeopardises love must be thrown overboard—certainly routine rules during a period of crisis, if the rules in question are not of fundamental importance.

However, if there is a basis of love and confidence, most teenagers will give at least a minimum of help—and with as much grace as one has a right to expect of them. For after all, nothing could be more untrue than the favourite remark of some parents: 'Well, washing-up's just as tiresome for me as for you isn't it?' The truth is that anything tiresome you do in your own house is a great deal less tiresome than it would be in someone else's. This goes for the teenage girl and her mother. A mother may feel that it *is* her daughter's home, as much as it is the parent's—her own bedroom to keep tidy, her own meals to clear away and wash up. But the daughter sees it in quite another way. It is her parent's house, her parent's sink, her parent's garden.

So when you rightly call your sons and daughters to the sink, remember that it's much more boring for them even than it is for you. It's up to you to shed a little radiance over the scene. Don't feel aggrieved if *they* insist on looking glum. Take it on yourself to start the conversation going. Make it your business to keep it going till the last plate is in the rack. It's a good tip to thank your helpers and send them off a little while before the final touch is put to the kitchen. The order of release is received with extra gratitude.

Housework should always be made as sociable as possible. I know a wise old lady who has trained a long string of girls in the domestic arts. Her recipe for success is *Do everything together*. She always works in pairs, never taking one room herself and leaving the teenager to 'get on with it' alone in another. I have often seen the two of them together washing clothes in a small hand-basin that was hardly adequate for one alone to use comfortably. But they both obviously felt that the sudden slops of soapy water into their shoes were well worth it. For they were the small price they paid for sociability and a shared experience.

It is true that some children of a rather more sophisticated type would react unfavourably to what they regarded as artificial matiness. In their case, it is better to give them sole responsibility for the clearing-away and washing-up on certain days and complete freedom for the rest. Whichever type of children you are blessed with, avoid one thing at all costs. Never allow a period to develop, say between the ages of seven and ten, when they are absolutely free from all responsibilities at home. This is in fact the very time when you will be tempted to concede precisely that liberty. By seven they will probably have forgotten the thrill of tying on Mum's apron and scattering the detergent in the bowl with generous abandon. Instead, their overriding instinct is to rush away from the table the moment they have swallowed the last mouthful, to revel in the beckoning world outside. But once you let this mad, joyous flight become a habit it will be extremely difficult to change it a few years later and make them stop behind to give you the help you need. As with all training, the secret is continuity. Pressures so gentle, gradual and familiar that they are scarcely felt.

I think there is a lesson here for us mothers when we face the problem of how to get teenagers to help. Apart from the particular technique described above, one point stands out. Make it clear that you value your teenager's *company* even more than her extra pair of hands.

Keeping a Close Relationship

This point raises the whole problem of intimacy between parents and their teenage children, particularly girls. It is only too easy for parents to begin treating their older children with detachment—both mental and physical. They notice that the children have become secretive during the last few years. Confidences are no longer freely offered. When asked for, they are either withheld or given grudgingly and as briefly as possible. It seems, then, that the children themselves want to change over to a detached and cool relationship with their parents.

Yet parents who are misled by superficial appearances and allow their teenagers to live in splendid isolation, may unwittingly cause immense damage. There was a case some years ago in a Juvenile Court, which attracted a good deal of attention at the time and still has a lesson for modern parents, even though the advice given by the magistrate might today be expressed in slightly different language. A girl of sixteen who had been travelling by tube without paying her fare, was up before the magistrate, who happened to be celebrated criminologist Professor Barbara Wootton (now Baroness Wootton), a woman of deep sympathies and immense experience.

'Go home and cuddle your daughter,' said Lady Wootton to the girl's mother, after she had put the girl on probation for a year; 'She is not too old to be cuddled.' Then Lady Wootton turned to the girl. 'You think you are not loved. That is not so.'

The difficulty had been that the mother had long ago given up expressing her genuine love for her daughter in any physical form.

'Do you ever cuddle your daughter?' asked Lady Wootton.

'Good heavens, no. She's much too big. . . . The thought never entered my head.'

We might be more inclined today to talk of putting our arms round an older girl and giving her a hug. But the point is the same.

Which do *we* follow, the mother or the magistrate? My own reaction when I first read the story was this. I'd find it very hard suddenly to begin hugging a girl who had reached her later teens. But it's natural and altogether different if you've never left off since she was born. Of course the magistrate was right. But she was setting that particular mother a most difficult problem: how to renew the physical expression of love after a gap of many years.

Such a poignant problem need never come the way of most of us. But on one condition. That we parents never allow our love for our children to become 'strong and silent'—*unexpressed*. To wish our children well is not enough. They must *feel* that we wish them well.

There is only one way to make sure of this. Make your love visible. Children see things in a very concrete way. To them, people who love, kiss. And if people don't kiss—then they don't love.

One can sympathise with the parent who lets physical endearments lapse at the teenage stage. Perhaps her daughter is already inches taller than herself. So many daughters are these days. How can you be expected to take her on your lap, as you did when she was little? Not only that, if you have younger children in the family still at a stage to be kissed and hugged quite naturally, you will hardly even notice that you have fallen out of the habit with your eldest. And then, how hard to begin again! There is only one easy solution. Recognise before teenage is reached that physical love will still be necessary. Never cease to give it.

Borrowing

Here is another prolific source of trouble. Children, especially girls, admire their parents' belongings at a very early age. Later they covet them. Then they 'borrow' them. An anecdote from Scunthorpe aptly illustrates the first stage of this process.

'My four-year-old daughter was watching me putting make-up on. "What is that for?" she asked. "To look nice," I replied. Minutes later, when I called her, she came out of the bedroom with powdered face and lipstick. "What did you do that for?" I asked angrily. "To look nice," she said smiling.'

A London mother sprayed her coat with scent before going out to a party. 'I went back to kiss my child, before going to bed. I found that she had used all my perfume over her clothes, and she exclaimed, "Oh, I smell like a garden now. All the fairies will visit me tonight in bed."'

I always allowed Catherine (as the youngest daughter) to be around when I was getting ready for a party. She loved to act as 'dresser' and when I was safely zipped up she would turn to her own adornment. She made herself look like an oriental princess, glittering all over. A place was even found for earrings—hooked through the button-holes of her dressing-gown.

You may object that this was just encouraging her to borrow without permission when she reached her teens. It did not work out that way. Teenagers who from childhood have been welcome in their mother's room are less likely to feel envy and resentment than those who have been kept at arm's length. They will be familiar with their mother's treasures, and know what they may and may not borrow. A mental pattern of borrowing mother's things *with permission* will be firmly established; instead of the opposite tactic of furtive and guilty forced-loans.

Anyway, a certain amount of borrowing is inevitable. My teenagers have at one time or another borrowed almost everything I possess, from toothpaste to typewriter. I have discovered it is best on the whole to overlook it. Borrowing seems to be an occupational disease of teenagers, and despite the inconvenience it sometimes causes must be endured for the sake of 'good relations'. As I have already stressed, nothing is worth the risk of a real scene and break in affection between parents and teenagers. But I do try to insist on one rule: The borrowed object must be returned before I need it.

It may be as well to add a note on borrowing for the benefit of parents who have children in their teens but are themselves in what my son Patrick calls euphemistically 'the early afternoon of life', i.e. any age from thirty-five to ninety. Borrowing may still seem to us older parents a somewhat reprehensible activity, never to be encouraged and only tolerated under duress. Frankly, this attitude will not do today. A great change has taken place since we were children ourselves in the attitude of the young towards borrowing. They are more generous in lending things to one another than we ever were. Their lack of a grasping property-sense seems to me admirable in many ways. No one hesitates to ask for the loan of a dress, coat or hat for a special occasion. Anyone who owns a fabulous hat can be sure it will go to many weddings—on a lot of different heads. Let us hope that possessiveness will not return to this generation in a great wave after they are married, changing them back into a new race of Soames Forsytes. But that is a matter for the future. At the moment, it is right for parents to conform to some extent to their children's ethics, particularly when these ethics are warm and generous. Mothers must never appear less liberal than their children's contemporaries and friends.

Pocket-Money

This is a subject of perennial discussion among parents. We are forever comparing notes, trying to discover the ideal sum to give our children which will neither stint nor spoil them. When I hear a parent ask, 'Is 2s … 10s … 15s … a week enough?', I want to ask in return, 'Enough for what?'

No hard-and-fast rules can be laid down about these money matters. So much depends on the circumstances of the parents, the claims of other members of the family, the way in which the teenager spends his allowance, etc. But on the whole it is wise to try to allow him roughly the same as his friends. We've all learned, as parents, to dread the teenager's typical refreain: 'But Daddy, *all my friends* have one … do it … go there …' All the same, the above rule is not a bad one to follow—always provided you approve of the friends!

Trouble with Younger Brothers and Sisters

Hostilities often break out between teenagers and the younger members of the family. The teenager, as one mother put it to me, 'is hateful to the younger children'. Bossy, impatient, sarcastic. The younger ones retaliate. They persist in treating the teenager as 'one of the children'. They resent his or her new-found dignity. Even more they resent the teenager's privileges. Particularly tiresome is their attitude to boy- or girl-friends—a mixture of ribaldry and curiosity. They will stop at no lengths of mischief. Eavesdropping on the telephone extension becomes a minor hobby. They even give their iniquity away by quoting samples of endearments thus overheard. When he was twelve Paddy inadvertently addressed a girl-friend as 'Honeysuckle'. He was never allowed to forget it by his hidden audience of giggling younger sisters.

Rule for parents: If in doubt, uphold the teenagers. They are more vulnerable, more touchy, and more in need of support.

It would be wrong to end this section on a note of gloom. For there is a very different side to the Teenager-Younger Children relationship from the one just described. Once the teenage girl is accepted as a semi-grown-up, no one is more popular with her younger sisters. Her hair-do and make-up are even more fascinating to watch than Mother's. It is an immense privilege to help set her hair, choose her jewellery for the evening, listen to her record-player. The same applies to the teenage boy. A man may not be a hero to his valet, but a boy is certainly a hero to his younger brother. In fact, from the younger children's point of view, the advantages of a teenager in the home far outweight the disadvantages of occasional criticism and bossiness. The only ticklish period is the time when the teenager is changing over from lower to higher status—and the small fry are unwilling to admit it. This transitional period must be speeded up in the interests of all. The parents are the people to do this. By firmly backing up the teenagers and insisting on their new position in the family, the parents will be fulfilling one of the many diplomatic tasks which come their way as the family grows up.

The Outside World — Two Extreme Attitudes

'Problem teenagers' have two opposite ways of puzzling their parents when it comes to mixing with the great world. They mix too much, or they do not mix at all. Either they are too shy to go to parties, or they think of nothing else.

If they are shy, don't force them to go to dances. If you do, they will only spend listless hours hanging around the food and drinks or chatting up the lady who looks after the coats. Give them, instead, hobbies and interests. Friends are made more easily by doing things together than by deliberately looking for them.

But if your teenagers are party-mad? Try at all costs to keep in touch with them and their friends. See that some of the parties, at least, are centred on your home. Concentrate first on birthdays and special occasions. Then, when your teenagers have got used to bringing their friends home, give them a room to themselves and let them enjoy it.

Of course, if you have been clever enough to start asking in your children's friends since they were quite small you will have no difficulty in establishing contacts when teenage arrives. Once again, it is a case of starting early and of starting the way you mean to go on. So we should begin entertaining friends of our five-year-olds. Then we'll have no trouble in getting them at fifteen to do their entertaining at home. Indeed, in these free and easy days there is sometimes the contrary danger of parents being put upon. I remember one mother describing her experiences with comical despair. In order to lure her children's teenage friends into her home she had spent back-breaking hours in the kitchen devising elaborate savouries and iced drinks. The net results were all too successful. There was no hanging back. Everything was gobbled up, there were repeated calls for replenishments and requests for plenty more parties under her hospitable roof. She decided teenagers were misunderstood. Far from being shy creatures of the wild, difficult to attract indoors, they were cheerful locusts.

I hope she went on with the parties, but made them cut their own sandwiches.

21

New Problems

'My fifteen-year-old asked for two Christmas presents. A glamorous nightie and—lacrosse boots! On Christmas morning she insisted on parading in both at once.' This mother has caught the real essence of the teenager. Child and adult—both at once.

In this particular case the schoolgirl managed to combine two attractive and innocent features, one from each of her worlds. Let her have her boots and nighties, bless her! But parents are not always so lucky in their fifteen-year-old's fancies. It may be a wish to combine work-shyness, which is not reprehensible in a small child, with heavy smoking, which cannot be called exactly reprehensible in an adult. Her own parents may do it. But both laziness and smoking are deplorable in a schoolchild. Or it may be something distracting and bad for schoolchildren, like grown-up sex; or bad both for adults and children, such as drug-taking.

At this point today's parents enter a world of complexity and danger which their own parents did not have to face. Anyone whose children were already grown up by the last third of the twentieth century must feel sympathy with the rising generation of parents. What with fall-out for babies and drugs, drinks, smokes and sex for adolescents, they have a hard row to hoe. Washing machines don't make up to them for the loss of security and ease of mind.

In touching upon these very serious problems during their earliest stage (i.e. as they affect the schoolchild rather than the student or young worker) I want to make one crucial point right away. The parents are still in command. But they will not be able to use their command effectively, nor even to remain in command at all, unless they get their own minds clear. One can't blame them for being at first somewhat vague about the rights and wrongs of such novel visitors to the schoolroom as soft drugs and hard sex. It is impossible for them not to hope that in their particular case they will never have to make the mental and moral effort of sorting it all out and deciding where to draw the line; that *their* son will never need, or feel he needs cannabis, or their daughter an abortion. Nevertheless the effort must be made. Social changes work faster than the normal parental processes. By the time we have cleared our own minds there may already be several young marijuana smokers among our children's friends. So let's look at drugs first.

The Primrose Path

I hope you agree for a start with those who think soft drugs lead on to hard, and that therefore drugs as such must be avoided. (Of course the transition is far from inevitable; but it occurs quite often enough.) If you do not agree, your problem is that much easier. But your children's will be more difficult.

I only knew of one persuasive argument against the view that soft leads on to hard and both must therefore remain illegal. Namely, that if young people could buy marijuana as effortlessly as they now buy cigarettes, they would be quite content to smoke it, and never stray into circles where heroin, cocaine and the amphetamines are pedalled. How much truth is there in this view?

It might work in some cases. But on the whole I don't trust it. It seems to me to be found on a fallacy. The fallacy that children only get into 'hard' trouble by accident. That it is nothing but the sheer accidental proximity of the market for 'pot' to the market for heroin (both being today illegal) that enables the heroin-pusher to do his disastrous job. Like a child who has to walk home from school every day along a tow-path, and accidentally falls one day into the river. Is that really how the young heroin addict gets hooked?

On the contrary, it is very often through the deliberate intention of the youngster himself to relieve adolescent depression by taking stronger and stronger drugs. Children who have taken to the regular smoking of 'pot' have not usually been remarkable, poor things, for their well-balanced, happy lives. The same emotional pressures, such as unhappiness at home, a failed love-affair, or a feeling of general frustration, which drove them to soft drugs, would soon move them on to something more potent. Not always; but too often. Even though marijuana itself may not be physically habit-forming, it forms a habit: a habit of using drugs to lift gloom. Whether or not soft drugs are more or less harmful than tobacco or alcohol is still an open question. The experts differ. Leaving that aside, I feel parents should do everything in their power to make sure their children are not taking any drugs. What can they do?

It is one of the blessings of this era that young people have a passion for discussion. Give them a chance and they will argue the hind leg off a donkey. In the case of discussions about drugs, the donkey is generally the parent. For the young usually manage to keep calm and reasonable despite the inflammatory nature of the subject, while their agonised parents make fools of themselves by going off the deep end. It might be thought unwise of parents to embark on an argument where they are likely to feel so strongly that they lose their heads and let the wrong side win. But self-control comes with practice. What would be fatal would be not to take advantage of youth's talkativeness. Their saving grace is their willingness to argue frankly and fully with anyone, young or old, male or female, high or low. They won't accept dictation—but they love discussion. My own generation was a great deal more secretive than my children's. In my youth it was a major problem to get children to tell adults what they really felt; now it's a major problem to halt them. We parents ought to make the most of our children's volubility. They may argue against us but at least they are hearing the point of view we hope will eventually convince them. I know a journalist who was converted from Communism to Christianity by the very book he had set out to demolish in a review.

The eagerness of children for discussion is often greater still with teachers, interviewers, even social workers, than with their own parents. Kay is a young girl who had started taking drugs at fifteen. She is now, alas, an addict, but trying to get cured. She had been unhappy at home (though very fond of her parents) and had moved along the primrose path from soft to hard drugs. But she is not uninterested in other people. One day she began discussing lesbianism with Margaret, a social worker. In the course of conversation it suddenly struck Kay that Margaret, a woman of forty, was unmarried.

'Margaret, are *you* a lesbian?'

The social worker laughed heartily in reply. She was one of those who recognised that the familiarity and frankness of the young are far removed from cheek, and make them easier to help than their reserved elders. That is why parents can meet the drug menace with determination if not absolute confidence. There is nothing they cannot talk out with their children today—on two conditions. First, that their own convictions are clear. Second, that the overall relationship is a happy one. I have tried in the first part of this chapter to show what one parent's convictions are. Elsewhere in this book there is a good deal about getting good relationships. Now we must go on.

Loving

Sex is in one way harder than drugs for a parent to cope with, and in another less difficult. Harder, because social habits and opinions on this subject are changing so rapidly that many parents scarcely know what they themselves think, let alone how they are going to advise their children. Easier than drugs, because sex is unlikely to endanger your child's life. An over-energetic indulgence in sex, with ups and downs of longing and disappointment, will certainly interrupt his or her education by preventing concentration and creating a disturbed atmosphere. Also, quite young children get V.D. these days. Quite young parents suddenly find they must take a grandchild into the family or organise an adoption. But V.D. is curable. And you can always prevent the latter by firmly putting your daughter on the pill. My youngest son, who knows I am a feminist, thought that I might be in favour of the pill solution, since it seems to produce at long last complete equality between women and men, girls and boys. He was wrong. Nevertheless it might appear at first sight to be a logical and even a necessary development.

An extremely conscientious parent of my acquaintance sent her youngest daughter to a mixed boarding-school. Having equipped Jane with the requisite number of skirts, shoes, hand-kerchiefs and pyjamas, she added a contraceptive. I think the coil. In view of that parent's high intelligence, I am quite sure she had visualised the *immediate* logical and almost inevitable result of her action—though she may not have foreseen what might be the final consequences. The immediate result could hardly be anything else but sexual inter-course at school for Jane. Perhaps Jane was a highly sexed child who would have had it anyway, *and* an unwanted baby. Perhaps, on the contrary, she was not really so sexy as her mother supposed. It is hard to be sure about these things. But once the coil was decided upon, Jane was pretty well bound to have sex. A toddler who is put into a life-jacket sooner or later plops into the pool. You expect him to and he knows it. It might be retorted that you don't *expect* your house to catch fire just because you invest in a fire-extinguisher. It's purely a safety measure, a last resort.

I don't accept this reply as valid. After all a fire is a very disagree-able affair. One takes a great many other steps besides buying an extinguisher to prevent the house being burnt down. One makes sure the electric cooker is turned off, the iron and T.V. set unplugged, the guard put round the fire. Sex, on the contrary, is not a nasty affair but a very agreeable one. If nothing whatever is done to hinder it, but instead it is made quite safe, there is every reason for the child to enjoy a series of lovely blazes.

My next point is to face the fact that many mothers today will posi-tively welcome an early blaze of sex, in their daughters. That Jane and Jenny and Joanna are all going to have love-affairs before marriage in no way worries them. It is just what they want. Why? For one thing, there are a good many rags and remnants of crude feminism lying around today. Out of the old rag-bag has come the belief that men have always enjoyed an unfair advantage over women, since they were able to live with girl after girl without having to bear the unhappy consequences. Now, runs the argument, the coil and the pill have given women the same advantages and happiness as men.

But is it happiness? Surely that is the key question. Yet few women ask it and even fewer follow it up. How many self-indulgent men are truly happier than those who use restraint? Of course no one likes the word promiscuity. It is indignantly rejected. That is not what we are after, is the universal cry. Mothers who plan to equip their schoolgirls with the pill probably envisage no more than half-a-dozen full-blown love-affairs before they meet the man they marry. Each one is to be a serious relationship, leading to a valuable step-by-step development of the immature lover into the emotionally complete young adult. (The possibility that intense affairs may end in painful breaks, straining or damaging the youthful personality, is evaded. So is the unpalatable fact that Romeo and Juliet were not trying to get O-levels.) Leaving aside the complicated question of whether sophisticated sex brings immediate happiness to the young or not, what about the long run? Parents should ask themselves this question. Are the happiest marriages those which come at the end of a road pitted by experiments conducted with the help of discarded and forgotten partners? Or those where the trials are made and borne together by the permanent partners, becoming an integral part of the complex thing called love? Apart from that question, it's as well to realise that every love-relationship is new and individual. A love-affair that is over has not necessarily prepared you for the one that follows, as an elementary course in typing or driving gets you ready for the advanced one. Indeed, there are several ways in which it can set you back. We heard recently of a 'female Casanova' who came to regret the 'dispersal of personality' caused by her way of life. She had left a bit of herself behind with each love and was in the end unable to reassemble herself as a complete woman. Again, the memories of past affairs linger on into marriage. They are just as likely to do harm as good. No lover has every possible perfection. Happy marriage is not improved by wishing one's husband or wife had some of the endearing little ways of his or her predecessors. Our children will not perform better as husbands or wives because of previous experience. They may *choose* better. But that is an argument in favour of later marriage, not of pre-marital sex.

A favourite reply to those like myself who would persuade children to keep sex until marriage, is based on the researches of Dr Kinsey. Most of us were probably surprised to learn that man's peak potency occurred at the age of sixteen. It was made to seem illogical that a boy should wait for sex until his powers were beginning to decline. 'Let children begin sex when nature itself decrees.' That is false logic.

How often do we listen to nature's decrees when they don't suit us? Nature has decreed that a girl shall be capable of having a baby every year or so from twelve or thirteen onwards until she is worn out. Rightly we ignore this biological decree. All our daughters' early fertility we devoutly hope will be wasted. With the same confidence we can ignore Dr Kinsey on behalf of our sons.

As I see it, there is a real and remorseless logic in the schoolgirl-on-the-pill syndrome which parents who advocate it fail to follow up. When all schoolgirls are on the pill, chastity will no longer be a dirty word. It will be a non-word. Marriage, in the present sense of a bond of faithfulness voluntarily and permanently joining together one man and one woman, will become another non-event. After that, what will become of the family? Redundant. And when the family has gone there will be no home.

A brilliant journalist, Mr Paul Johnson, recently predicted that a hundred years hence people would be living in a society from which the family had disappeared—since women would no longer choose to bear children within their own bodies when they could be comfortably incubated in laboratories. The forward-looking author found nothing much wrong with this brave new world. His only fear was lest universal participation in government, through computered registration and communication of our smallest desires, should put an end to privacy in the home. What home? Why does the writer think there would still be homes after families had vanished? The wheel would have come full circle, with mankind back to his original state of a roving animal, maybe a little above the herring which never meets his mate or knows his own progeny, but below the partridge who mates for life.

Most parents are not much worried about the next hundred years. But they *are* confused and anxious about what is said to happen today. Is it really true that if their daughters are not seen living with a man, or at any rate have not had the experience, they will feel out on a limb? In that case it may seem hard on one's own child to train him or her to behave so differently from the majority. It certainly would be hard if the parents themselves were only half convinced about the truth of what they were urging upon their children. That is why I have made such a plea for parental clarity, before the time comes to advise their growing sons and daughters.

To sum up. There are three possible positions for the modern parent to consider.

First, sincere belief in complete sexual freedom and absence of all restraint. This should undoubtedly involve the earliest possible use of contraceptives. Personally I think that such procedure is bad for the individual and calamitous for the community. But I recognise that people whom I respect in other ways do in fact adopt it. All I can say to them is, think again.

Second, there is the religious belief. That sex and marriage are intended to be sacred, even if they do not always work out that way. If you hold these views you are fortunate indeed. Nevertheless, your course in helping your children to share them will not be all plain sailing. To tell fifteen-year-olds nothing else but that something is *wrong* when they know their friends actually do it, or at any rate project it, is too simple for this generation. Unless of course they go to schools where they only meet others with the same upbringing. Even then it is taking a risk.

I suggest that parents should discuss the subject thoroughly with their children as a matter of consuming human interest, whatever their views, backing up their religious arguments with some of those I have mentioned above. Parents whose own marriage has some conscious spiritual content are not usually the ones who have been unlucky and made a really hideous mess of it. As advisers, therefore, they are in a fairly strong position. Another point can be added which I find makes no great impact on those without an ethical code but is none the less true, and a great help to people who can accept it. This is, that faithful love within marriage brings infinite compensations, *even in the purely sexual sphere*, for the renunciation of variety, novelty and all the rest of it. That is not surprising. The secret of life lies in selection. Selection is compulsory all along the line. In sex, with the best will in the world you can't sleep with every attractive person you meet. Even after a life-time's zealous labour in the sexual field only a tiny fraction of the possibles will actually have been notched up. The better way is to select one, confident that in this perfected experience all others will be mirrored and magnified.

Third, there is a position somewhere between the two already described, a position blurred by uncertainty but tinged with hope. It is occupied, I can't help feeling, by a large number of parents. Many of them are aware of failures in their own past. Despite this, they hope their children will be luckier. But how to help these children is a question to which they don't know the answer. As a result, they decide not to interfere, they avoid prying or making enquiries, and they accept in a civilised way whatever comes. This may be peaceful but it is not parenthood. Others in this group feel they have been successful in their own marriages but more through accident than any principle they have followed. That feeling also leads to non-interference in their children's lives. Others again in this group would like to see their children pursue a course midway between absolute freedom and complete restraint. Just the right number of affairs before marriage and no more. That solution is of course purely pragmatic. No one can decide in advance what is the right number, least of all the parents. All they can do is to be sympathetic when things go wrong and try not to be too 'old-fashioned' when pre-marital affairs go right. Like the father who agreed with his wife that their daughter should be supported in every way if she decided on pre-marital sex. But when she brought her first boy-friend home, and when the boy-friend plonked down his suitcase in their daughter's bedroom, and when they both came down together to breakfast next morning—the father had an uncontrollable longing to reach for the horse-whip. Which was at fault, his theory or his instinct?

In all these types of intermediate positions, parents have a duty to think out their views afresh. You may then decide—and I hope you will—that our present permissive society has not, after all, found all the keys to happiness. After that you must say so to your children. There may be a few awkward moments. 'Mummy, did you practice what you preach?' You don't *have* to answer; like the teacher who was asked in the middle of a biology class whether she used contraceptives herself, and went straight on with the membrane of the uterus, sweeping the question aside. But there is a lot to be said for admitting, as a parent, that one has made mistakes and changed one's mind.

22

A Later Stage of Discipline

Fortunately our teenage children need help over many matters less perplexing and thorny than sex. Our problem as parents is to help them make a successful transition from the child's world as a whole, to the adult's, and at the same time make a success of being a fourteen or fifteen-year-old. The question I shall try to answer in this chapter is: Can we help them *directly* in the multitude of smaller things which concern their welfare, by issuing a clear-cut 'do' or 'don't'—in other words by discipline. We may not feel sure whether or not to tolerate teenage sex; we know quite well that too little sleep or not enough washing are intolerable. Should discipline be enforced?

'We learn from suffering', said the ancient Greeks. In one sense children of all ages can by convinced by their own hard experience. The exceptions are when they may be tempted literally or metaphorically to play with fire—matches or marijuana—where the experiment would be positively dangerous. In the case of matches, babies must learn from authority, the parent using a judicious mixture of 'don't' and putting the match-box out of reach. With drugs one prays they will be prepared to learn from someone else's experience; the press, books, television, conversations with doctors, parents or their own contemporaries. But where there is no danger, a child learns better from having his own way and taking a knock. The process of course begins long before the teens. From Cardiff comes the story of a three-year-old, already up against a problem that will haunt him right into his teens, and beyond. How to repair a mistake without admitting one has made it. How to accept good advice without seeming to have budged an inch.

This child's mother warned him that it was too cold to play out-doors. But he insisted he was quite warm and went on standing sentry at the garden gate. 'At last he ran in,' writes his mother, 'telling me it was not because he was cold, but his gun was, and he must give it a warm!' Can we persuade a teenager to take advice when even a toddler seeks for—and finds—a way round?

We have already seen in previous chapters that the technique of discipline changes at teenage, though the actual year will vary from child to child. The accent is on co-operation in normal cases. Results should be obtained by consulting your teenager rather than by ordering him.

It is true, of course, that in all problems which are likely to crop up you must try to keep a leap ahead. Rough out in advance your own answers to questions of money, holidays, friends, homework and work in the home—the two last being rivals for the schoolchild's time which can be played off against one another by your ingenious son. 'Mummy, I couldn't clear away, I had too much homework.' And at school: 'I couldn't finish my prep, Mummy needed help.' After planning in advance, work out the details in collaboration with him.

Make a big switch from 'don't' to 'do'. When you see him at a loose end—loose ends multiply at this age for your son has an instinctive fear of getting 'tied up', of losing his freedom—don't just tell him to stop hanging about wasting his time. Find him a group to join, a game to play, a piece of altruistic work to do for a cause outside himself, a hero to imitate.

Even when you have relegated 'don't' to an unimportant place in your vocabulary and embarked on a positive policy, your switch is not complete. Too much 'do this' or 'do that' is no more acceptable to the adolescent than the old 'don't'. So try changing your orders into suggestions. If he turns them down—and he is not obliged to say Yes to a suggestion as he should to a command—think of another. It is hard work being a parent. One is always racking one's brains for new ideas: thinking of new answers to the eternal question, 'Can you suggest anything …?'

It is not always possible, however, with the greatest tact and the best will in the world, to avoid some kind of clash with your teenager. Not all orders can be made more palatable by being presented as expendable suggestions. Not all 'don'ts' can be discarded. A teenager, for instance, must not be allowed to waste his time and his parents' or the country's money, by slacking at school. How is discipline to be applied in a case like this?

Is There Still a Place for Physical Punishment?

Some years ago it looked as if the young were moving back to a belief in the old disciplines based on physical pain. Schoolchildren, we read, were voting for the cane—I had quite a number of letters from young people advocating a return to corporal punishment. Here is a letter from a young hospital nurse, claiming that she herself had been cured of chronic idleness by what she called a 'strapping'.

'At school I was always in trouble. Prep. schools were allowed to deal in their own way with us; male or female, you got the strap. But then came college or high school. Boys continued to get a strapping but we girls got "lines". I regret to say I must have written almost the complete works of Shakespeare as forms of punishment. But did it do me any good? No! It did not. In the end I had to be sent up before the rector. There I got my choice: either I learnt my lesson from the "line" punishment, or else I should get the strap. Needless to say, I did get the strap; but the ignominy of being the only girl in school to get a strapping taught me my lesson. And I've been made a better person for it, because I've never forgotten that episode.'

This young woman goes on to say that she herself would invoke the same methods of discipline, were she ever in the same position, 'to get a good result'. She winds up with this general remark: 'May I say, as a last bite at the present generation, both parents and children: this would be a better world if parents commanded respect from their children. If it can't be done without the rod—and I know that is the case with many families—then for any sakes, use it. Perhaps,

who knows, it might even cut down the amount of child delinquency there is in the world today.'

That's a thoughtful letter, whatever we may think of its conclu-
sions. But now I want to pose a question. Which cured this teenager?
Strap or ignominy? Surely the mental smart not the physical blow.
The latter jolted her out of her idle rut. It had 'startle' value. Such
disciplinary action might work once, in special cases. But it cannot
be repeated nor applied far and wide.

With normally tough children, a few repetitions of the treatment
and familiarity would breed contempt. The strap would no longer
produce a feeling of ignominy. There would remain only a slight
fear of physical pain, and relief that it would so soon be over. Then—
happy idleness again!

With sensitive children, a strapping is the wrong kind of punishment altogether. It may do them untold mental harm. As for the
person who administers the punishment—he is possibly right when
he says, 'it hurts me more than it hurts you'. But not, perhaps, in
the way he imagines. The man with the cane may injure his own
character. There is enough sadism (where sex is said always to play a
loathsome part) left in civilised man to make it unsafe and unfair to
put temptation in his way.

There is another reason why I cannot accept this solution to
the problem of discipline. It is because of the able letter in which
it is offered. This girl shows herself at twenty to be a responsible
person, interested in juvenile delinquency and parents' duties. I do
not believe the seeds of public spirit were implanted purely by that
strap. They were already there in her, even at sixteen. Admittedly the
'lines' did not make them germinate. But could nothing else have
been found more subtle than 'lines' or a beating, boredom or force? I
suspect that the giving of more responsibility in school and perhaps
at home too would have been the true solution. Often the best way
to cure black sheep is to put them in positions of trust.

Should We Humiliate Them?

A Warrington father deliberately chooses *humiliation* as the best method of enforcing discipline. 'When I punish, the offender has to bring the rod from the place where it hangs. I find the humiliation of having to do this is a strong deterrent.'

This suggestion provoked several heated outbursts from correspondents. Here is a characteristic one. 'Please refer in future writings to the danger of humiliating children, and most especially by making them bring the cane. It is too terrible to think about and is the worst of all fearful cruelties. A child's life can be ruined. And the worst tragedy of it all is that the parent may not realise what he is doing. I had just such a parent and I am only now beginning to recover from convictions of inferiority at the age of thirty.'

In my own view, while it is often right to make a child ashamed of himself, it is always wrong to humiliate him. Shame springs from inner consciousness of guilt, and may be a necessary experience on the road to recovery. Humiliation is inflicted from outside. Literally, it means levelling someone to the ground. The last thing a parent should want to do is to undermine his child's self-respect. By making him feel a worm—a groundling—you may lower the teenager's standards instead of helping him to raise them. The safest rule is always: Aim to build them up, not to dress them down.

A Moral From Last Century

Just over a century-and-a-half ago a great battle was being fought. I don't mean Waterloo, though the battle I *am* thinking of was actually taking place at the same time. Whereas it took a matter of days to win the Waterloo campaign, the other battle dragged on for years. This was the fight to abolish brutal methods of discipline in the British army and navy, especially the cat-o'-nine-tails. Gradually the second battle was won also. Both savage crimes and brutal punishments began to disappear. Not because the cat had at last stamped out the criminals. But because both crime and punishment had been ameliorated by a better type of man entering the Services. Better educated, living in better conditions, and better cared for by his officers.

That principle is one of the laws of human nature. A good permanent response is never achieved by brutality but only by humanity. True, if a punishment is savage enough it may temporarily suppress or deflect crime. Young hooligans who roar into holiday resorts and beat up harmless visitors would no doubt find some other way of expressing themselves if they knew discipline was going to be applied in the form of 500 lashes (a common punishment for boy-soldiers who got drunk on duty in the old days, administered in the presence of a doctor and often in instalments, between visits to hospitals). But even this odious discipline, familiar to cinema audiences (*The Charge of the Light Brigade*) or a mini form of it, say, ten strokes of the birch, would not *cure* our hooligans. They must indeed be deterred, in my view by arrests and heavy fines; but cure will only be achieved by more responsible parents, the fruitful extension of the period of schooldays, and improved youth clubs. A telling point was recently made by Mr Ronald Goldman in his book called *Angry Adolescents*, an account of the near-miracle wrought by personal devotion in an English village infested by hooligans. He pointed out that 'A full-time youth leader in the village would have cost far less than the £4,750 spent on average each year in prosecuting, remanding, borstalising and imprisoning our worst members. But our annual grant for the club rarely came to more than £35!'

Incidentally, it is only education in some form which can protect and fortify the rising generation of adolescents against the violence they will inevitably see on television and cinema screens. If we could really protect our children by banning violence on the screen, I should be in favour of a total ban. I am afraid, however, enough violence will always creep in to injure potential delinquents. The only sure protection lies in the cultivation of an antidote within themselves. Something which makes them revolt against senseless destruction and cruelty.

Youth Speaks Out

During the last few years, despite increased rowdyism in some quarters, the more intelligent ranks of young people seem to have changed their minds again about the cane. We hear no more of votes to bring it back. But we do hear of decisions by prefects to abolish it where it still exists. This to me is an excellent sign. Schoolboys who vote in favour of abolition are to be congratulated. They are not such innocents as to imagine misbehaviour will vanish with the cane. Rules will still be broken and have to be enforced. But at teenage it is public opinion, i.e. the public opinion of their school world, which is the most effective force available. Provided of course that public opinion inside the school is on the side of law and order. It seems probable that in the next few years many silly and unnecessary rules will disappear, many day-to-day arrangements will be taken over by the children themselves, and the teachers will be left more time and spirit for their unique expertise—teaching.

Much of this goes for the home also. Older children should be invited to share in devising the family routine. If I had my time again I would be rather less permissive about nursery-stage unruliness and more sympathetic to hypercritical and difficult adolescents. The following complaint will not be heard in the one- or two-child family. But it is not uncommon among the older girls in the larger family: 'It's the little ones. . . . Their noise and quarrelling and bad manners get on my nerves. And the trouble is that when I'm at home I seem to slip back into my old self, and behave just as badly as the children, or worse. My mother sometimes tries to make me more tolerant by pointing out that when I was their age I had the same faults. Of course I know this. But the thought of it makes me even more irritated with them. I hate to see my own childish faults reproduced in them, more than I hate any others. I suppose it's because they remind me of what I want to forget. Or what I want to believe never happened!'

In cases like this the adolescent is undoubtedly hampered in her natural and rightful development by frustrations at home. It is very little good trying to discipline her tantrums by punishment. One delightful child I know ran away from her home in the north of England at the age of thirteen, with the eccentric idea of living with a school-friend's 'Gran' in the Midlands. From six to twelve years old this child had been extraordinarily helpful at home and good with her younger brothers and sisters. 'Quite a little mother to them', as her own mother said pathetically. Perhaps that was partly why the reaction came. An experienced social worker had to be called in, the child's mother was advised to give up going out to work despite a semi-invalid father and straightened circumstances, and the family settled down again. There was no one and nothing on which to fix the blame. Except perhaps the poverty still remaining among some large families. Thank heaven for the wisdom of welfare officers.

Start Training Early

One last point. Teenage discipline, to be really successful, begins long before teenage. In all kinds of training that deals with living things we find the principle is the same. Start right, start early, and keep it up. No one who was training young trees would dream of leaving them to spread and straggle, unfed and untended for years, and then hope to get good results by a sudden sharp pruning and lavish doses of fertiliser. It is better to prune late than never to do it at all, but the results of early neglect will always be visible.

So with the training of children. It begins, to be exact, with the parents themselves, before the children are born. Let them clarify their own ideas of right and wrong. So many adults have but the haziest notions of their own code. Is there any harm in skipping off a bus without paying the fare? Are they going to ask for half-fares for their children when they are over fourteen just because they happen to be small for their age? They have not thought out their ideas of right and wrong. Then how can they teach? Parents, clear your own decks!

Next, they must transmit their code clearly and firmly. No letting up or weak indulgence for the sake of peace and quiet. The years before teenage, not teenage itself, should be the tough time. As a correspondent from London puts it, whose daughter is now about to enter her teens: 'I have been a strict but loving parent, and now I can see the fruits of my training. The going was tough, constantly teaching her right from wrong. Many friends thought I was hard; but now when they praise her and invite her out all over the place, I feel proud.' And her daughter's comment, during the thick of this tough, pre-teenage period? 'You are the best Mummy and Daddy I have ever had!'

In a normal, happy family, where both parents have taken a hand in discipline from the word go, teenage should be an affectionate period rather than a 'firm one'. The years of most rigorous discipline should already be behind. Of course if those years have been eaten by the locusts and no consistent discipline applied, there may be serious trouble at teenage. Abnormal measures may be needed. But normally, teenage discipline takes the form of sympathetic guidance and advice from parents in close contact with their young sons and daughters. Trivial lapses should not now be dwelt on, at least not as pointedly as they would have been during the earlier training period. It is far worse to lose one's temper with a teenager for some minor but irritating offence than with a child of seven or eight. At all costs, affectionate relations must be maintained through these critical, sensitive years. The bread of love, cast upon the waters during stormy times, always comes back.

I will end with a quotation from the famous essayist and wit, Sidney Smith. He wrote before the stern Victorian papa was heard of, and long before our twentieth-century educationists had reacted against his despotic ways.

'We are convinced that those young people will turn out to be the best men, who have been guarded most effectively in childhood from every species of useless vexation, and experienced in the greatest degree of blessings of a wise and rational indulgence.'

These words seem to me both sage and beautiful. Once again we have to admit there is nothing new under the sun: the most we can hope for is to be the rediscoverers of truth.

23

Full Life or Family Life— Which Shall I Choose?

A mother recently described her ten-year-old daughter's favourite game of make-believe. 'She is a secretary and travels regularly, carefully ascertaining train times. Married to a "nice man" who allows her to continue her career, she is nevertheless a competent housewife. She has four children, because that is a nice number to play *Ludo*.'

In this child's fantasy we see many an adult dream come true. How sensible and natural it all sounds. To be a mother of four and keep your job at the same time! Surely every 'nice man' would 'allow' his wife to fulfil herself in this way? And surely every intelligent woman would choose to do so?

I believe the prevalent modern attitude in women is indeed 'to have it both ways' somewhat after the manner of this picture. To my mind this view is an advance on the 'progressive' ideas of twenty years ago, when a career was everything and a family took second place in the scale of ambitions. Personally I subscribe, on the whole, to the ideal outlined by the child above. But there are so many complexities involved in the whole question, so much loose thinking, so many half-truths and self-deceptions bandied about in current discussions of Motherhood versus a Career, that it is worth while trying to get a clear view of the *pros* and *cons* on each side.

To begin with, the argument starts on the assumption that motherhood in itself is not a career. This is true in a narrow economic sense. Men do not pay their wives for being mothers, nor, for that matter, for being housekeepers either. (Some people think they ought to. I do not agree, though I do believe that every wife should know her husband's income.)

Yet in another sense motherhood is a career, and a unique career. It is unique in two different ways which are so widely different as to seem almost contradictory. 1 It is the most *common* career a woman can choose. 2 It is the most uncommon of all careers, for no one but *one woman* can undertake it in any particular case.

What then are some of the special things that you, and you only, can give your children?

The Gift of Love

You can love them, and love them more completely than anyone else except their father.

You can also give *them* an opportunity for loving back. The importance of this aspect of love in children's lives is not always stressed as much as the other. Yet it is equally vital to their well-being. Children need to be the active givers of love, as well as its passive receivers.

But of course children will give their love to anyone who looks after them kindly, you say? I agree. They will love their nurses, crèche attendants, nursery-school teachers and all the other mother-substitutes who drift into their lives and drift out again. We must be profoundly thankful if they are able to find devoted people like these to be the objects of their love. But it will not be the same love as the love they would have given a mother. For one thing, it cannot in the nature of the case be so continuous and therefore so deep and pervading.

But it will not be quite the same towards *her*, either, if she is only a part-time mother, an in-and-out mother. The child's love may seem to be just as deep and strong at first as the love he would have felt towards a more devoted parent. For children do not like their idols to have feet of clay. They shut their eyes to it as long as possible. It is extraordinary how much love young children bear towards even the worst of parents. Becky Sharp, the villainess of Thackeray's *Vanity Fair*, was adored by little Rawdon her son—until he grew old enough to see the viper under the dazzling skin.

A mother who is a full-timer, at least until the child is four years old, gets a vision of perfect love that is more than exhilarating. It compensates a thousand-fold for any sacrifices she may have made in choosing motherhood as her sole career.

Thomas at three had heard the story of *Peter Pan* read aloud. One day he asked me, 'What was Wendy's mother called?' 'Mrs Darling,' I replied. 'You're my darling aren't you, Mummy?' said he. At the age of seven, when the war had just started, he suddenly said, 'Mummy, you are so brave!' 'Why?' I asked. 'Because you bear the merciless threats of life!' But perhaps the compliment that surprised me most came from seven-year-old Judith who had just started at a Convent school. In a burst of emotion she hit upon the highest term of praise she had learnt: 'Oh, you beautiful Virgin!'

A child who only sees his mother for a few of his waking hours cannot love with the fullness and abandon he needs. This is a great deprivation. Being unable to love completely may have as bad an effect on the child as not being loved enough. It may cause emotional and spiritual immaturity, and stunt the growth of his whole personality. In due time it may even prevent him from making a success of his own marriage.

The Gift of Religion

A child's religious life begins well before school age. He asks many pertinent and searching questions about religion at three or four years old, long before he is sitting in a class for religious instruction under a trained teacher. These questions crop up at all hours of the day—on walks, during meals, in the bath. They may easily start before three, if there are older children in the family.

The pre-school teacher on this, of all subjects, should not be anybody else but a parent. And that parent, throughout the day at least, is his mother.

I wish I could remember all the penetrating questions my under-fives have thought up on the nature of God. Thomas, at two-and-a-half, refused to say his grace one day. 'But don't you want to thank God

for your tea?' I asked. 'No,' he replied, 'I didn't like the cake He sent.'
There, surely, is a golden moment for a word of simple explanation.

Antonia at four, on the way up to bed, asked, 'Did God make
my tricycle?' 'No,' answered Thomas promptly, on my behalf. He
was interested in how things were made and did not want the factory to lose the credit. 'But God made the man who made the
tricycle,' retorted Antonia. A year later she suddenly leant over to
me in church and in an infinitely mysterious whisper, pronounced:
'Nobody knows who made God . . .' Here was another good chance
for later discussion about the meaning of Creation.

During the war Patrick, aged four, remarked as he ate his lunch,
'There isn't the same God for us and the Germans, is there, Mummy?'
It was evidently high time to start telling him about the universal
Fatherhood of God.

The Gift of Discipline

This is a difficult gift to impart and often an uncongenial one to
receive. It should come best from someone the child loves deeply, a
parent. And it should come from the earliest years, almost imperceptibly, so that the child grows up to feel it comes from *within* himself,
and not from outside.

Twenty years ago, when I was a young mother, we were given a
very simple rule for disciplining our children. We just had to give the
reason for everything we asked the child to do or not do. If a mother
failed to give a reason; or if the child disagreed with the reason she
had given; or if he just did not understand it—well, you could not
expect a self-respecting child to obey you. But once everything was
rationally explained, then, hey presto! the child would leap to obey!

As I suggested in an earlier chapter, it is indeed of the utmost
importance to make every effort to enlist the child's intelligent co-
operation in your 'do's and don'ts'. To make him 'see reason' when it
is a matter of obedience. But today I have come to believe that the
above account of discipline is only part of the story, and the easier
part at that.

Among other things, it disowns or disregards what theologians call 'original sin'—the instant that begins to show itself in every child from the age of about six onwards, to say to himself 'I know I ought to do it, but I don't *want* to—I *won't!*' There are really two points here. Discipline may mean somehow dispelling his insistent desire to do a certain thing despite the fact that *his own reason* tells him it is a silly thing to do, or a bad thing to do. Even more difficult, it may mean training him to do certain things without knowing exactly why, but simply because he is told to do them by a higher authority whom he loves and trusts. To obey the seemingly *irrational* is hardest of all, yet sometimes it must be done.

So if a mother can give her child this kind of discipline as well as the easier kind, she will have added a valuable stone to the foundations of his future. For the commands we are given by many higher authorities including Providence itself in later life, and which we *have* to obey, willy nilly, are often of this most difficult sort. We are made to accept losses of relations and friends for which we can see no reason. We ourselves appear to have 'bad luck' which seems inexplicable or even malevolent. But if we have been taught to accept what life sends us as from a higher authority we love and trust, without always demanding a clear reason for what occurs, we shall live to thank the teacher, and be happy.

The Gift of the Family

'Family feeling', or the sense of belonging to a living unit, dawns early even in quite a young child. In later life, especially during the strains and stresses of adolescence, this feeling of a secure framework will stand the child in good stead. My family are great critics of each other, and find plenty of time for disagreement. But they have a dramatic sense of 'the family'. When, during the holidays, all ten of us are sitting round the table together, one of the younger ones will often remark with intense satisfaction, 'Now the *whole family* is together.'

But this feeling is not born in them ready-made. It must be built up gradually by the facts themselves of family life, rather than by preaching about its value. Who can set 'family life' afloat in the first instance but the parents? As the children grow up, the task is carried on by older brothers and sisters. They gradually take on many semi-parental functions, allowing the younger ones to enter *their* solar system instead of remaining attached only to mother or father. Nothing has given me more satisfaction in the last few years than to see Antonia enthroned in her room, getting ready for a party, and surrounded by her attentive and fascinated sisters, Judith, Rachel and Catherine. Or to know that Michael and Kevin have gone off for the day to follow Patrick round the local golf course. Once the family is launched, family feeling will expand and develop on its own initiative. But I doubt if the start will ever be made, from which the rest grows, if there is an absentee mother.

Putting the Family First

So far I have not gone beyond the fact that motherhood is a career and a very great one. I have suggested that half-time or absentee mothers are likely to have less successful careers, *as mothers*, than full-timers would. But here many women may raise a strong objection. 'Surely a woman can have a family and an outside career—*provided she always puts her family first?*'

This seems to me to be the moment when most self-deception creeps into the argument. 'Family *and* career—with family as No. 1 priority' sounds such a simple solution. And it is only too easy to persuade oneself that because one wishes and intends to put one's family first, one is in fact doing so. My own experience is that the holding of this balance, with the scales always ready when necessary to tip over to the family side, is the most difficult thing in the world.

How far is it possible in practice to make a genuine career subordinate to family life? Family life seems of its nature flexible. Children's needs, apart from the really basic ones of food, clothing, house and education, are in a sense 'movable feasts'. You can so easily tinker about with household arrangements. You can change children's bedtimes and mealtimes within reason. You can say you will read to them and play with them double-time tomorrow, if you have to be out today. You can give them an extra holiday in an emergency, or send one somewhere 'for a treat'.

But you can't send your career for a holiday. You can't change office hours or let the boss off early 'as a treat'. Even if you have a career which allows you to suit your family, there is still something basically rigid about it. You hesitate to tamper with set times and appointments, unless it is absolutely essential. How much easier it is to switch the family about than the career.

So it needs great ingenuity and firmness as a mother, and not too great ambition as a career-woman, to make the compromise work. In fact, to make sure that your career really *is* subordinate to your family. Even then, with the best intentions in the world, you may not succeed. For careers have a way of encroaching; and the family, like a valuable plant growing in a garden among other more rampant species, is not always tough in asserting its rights.

Up till now I have restricted the discussion to general arguments concerning the family, and the mother's place in it. But it is time to focus attention more sharply. What have our children themselves to say on these points? What would they wish for themselves and for their mother? And quite apart from their expressed desires, what kind of solution would in fact be best for them?

24

Full Life or Family Life—Which Would my Children Choose for Me?

When Antonia and Thomas were quite young I used to go once a week to a Party meeting. 'Where are you going, Mummy?' they would ask. 'To the Labour Party.' 'Well, we don't like you going to parties and leaving us behind.' It was a double grievance—to miss a party *and* be left behind.

Another child, whose mother had to visit an ante-natal clinic regularly, took a similar dislike to these outings. 'Mummy, I like all my aunties except my Auntie Natal,' she said one day before the usual visit. 'Whatever do you mean?' asked her mother. She replied, 'You take me to see all my other aunties, but you never let me come with you to Auntie Natal!'

Stories like these, and many others which every mother could add from her own experience, leave very little room for doubt. As far as the children's *feelings* are concerned, the answer to the question put at the end of the last chapter is clear. Children want their mothers to be around all the time. They never want them to go away. They always protest when they do so. It may be all very unreasonable, but that's the way it is. Their instinct is perpetually to circle round us like small satellites circling round a sun. *We* may sometimes feel dizzy and exhausted. *They* feel safe and secure.

The other day I was taken aback by my six-year-old's reaction to what I regard as a very limited life 'outside the home'. He knows that I go to an office about once a week. Coming home and expecting me to be in, he found he'd forgotten it was 'office day'. 'Oh, bother,' he cried angrily, 'Mummy's *always* at the office!'

Mothers who are forced by economic circumstances to go out to work have no choice in the matter. Day nurseries are necessary in which they can leave their babies and know they are safe and well looked after. But personally I shall not feel we have achieved an ideal state of affairs in this country until no woman, through lack of an adequate family wage, is forced to go out to work while her children are still young.

How many of these working mothers would say their children *liked* the daily parting? A mother from Chatham writes revealingly: 'Paul, our three-and-a-half-year-old son, asked me why I had to go to work. I told him, to get pennies for his sweets, etc. Next morning he said, "You won't see me tomorrow. I'm going to London on my tricycle to get shillings for Mummy's gas."'

Incidentally, children are much more sensitive to grown-up worries than we sometimes think. Particularly to financial worries. So parents must be careful how they discuss these things in front of their children. A mother and father were moaning, half humorously, at breakfast over the iniquities of income tax. Their young daughter anxiously inquired what was the matter. 'It's the naughty Chancellor of the Exchequer,' explained her mother. 'He's trying to take away all Daddy's money.' The child began to worry continuously about their supposed plight. Her peace of mind and even her health were affected by this frightening question of what was going to happen to them all when Daddy had no money left.

Of course, children whose mothers do not go out to work often play the game of being the breadwinner—of keeping their parents instead of vice versa. But in their case the game is not tinged with anxiety or a wish to save Mummy from having to leave home every day. It will just be an amusing game, based on imitation of grown-up activities, or a desire to seem a 'big boy' instead of a little one.

Here is an instance of this kind from East Ham. 'My small son often dons his elder brother's cap and tells me he is off to work to get me some money. One hand is in his pocket and a "cigarette" of rolled paper in his mouth. He is always back with the explanation that the "works" have sold out of money, but will have some tomorrow.'

Children over five whose mothers go to work part-time, and who are left with people they trust, may accept the parting philosophically. But we must not be surprised if they produce some odd reasons for what is, to them, an odd situation. The following is the story of a South Wales mother whose five-year-old daughter interpreted her separation from her mother in an unexpected way. 'I am nursing in a large T.B. hospital. My little girl was being looked after by her school teacher. At tea-time she told the teacher's husband she could not go with her Mummy to the hospital as she might get T.V.'

Of course it is possible to bribe children into accepting their mother's absence with a good grace. I know one mother who went out to work in the mornings and promised her three-year-old son a magnificent tricycle for Christmas, as a result of her labours. I always wondered which he really would have enjoyed most, the eight-guinea tricycle or the mornings with his mother.

In my own case, if I had to be away from home for the night I used to bring back a tiny present for each child, known to the family as a 'surprise packet'. The thought of the surprise packet certainly softened their protests at my departure. Indeed, they have been known to inquire wistfully when I was next going away for the night. But obviously surprise packets are not a permanent basis for family life.

From the point of view, then, of the children's feelings—of their likes and dislikes—a part-time mother can rarely be their deliberate choice. This is unquestionably true of the first few years of the child's life. It is true in many cases even up to early teenage. When the children are at home themselves they like Mother to be at home too. I am continually surprised by the objections my older children make when I tell them I am going to be out for the evening. Or to put it the other way around, I am surprised at the satisfaction they express, when they hear I am going to be in; particularly as homework, followed closely by bedtime, generally prevents us from doing much together.

But the children's likes and dislikes are not the heart of this matter, though clearly they are a very important part of it. It is always possible that what they like best is not actually the best thing for them. A large number of mothers are today convinced that it is in fact better for children, even for children under official school age, to go to a nursery school rather than to remain with their mothers all day long.

A young woman once wrote to the *Daily Express*: 'At a Mother's Meeting I attended, an overwhelming majority voted in favour of nursery schools for children under school age because "it is better for the child" and "mothers should be free part of the time to express themselves". Because I prefer to look after my family myself while they are tiny, I was warned I shall be a possessive mother by the time I am forty!'

There are three separate points here:

1 'Nursery schools are good for children.'

2 'Freedom from their children is good for mothers.'

3 'Undiluted life with mother is bad for children later on, because the mothers become possessive.'

Let us look at these three arguments in turn.

1 *Are nursery schools the best thing for children under school age?* It sounds platitudinous to reply, 'This depends on the nursery school and also on the individual child.' But that is the truth. A nursery school which lasts a few hours in the mornings, or a percussion band or dancing class which takes place in the afternoon, may be of great benefit to four- and even three-year-olds. On the other hand, a day-nursery (which is not the same thing as a nursery school, but is often confused with it) which simply looks after a child's physical needs from dawn till dusk, is not generally 'better for the child' than the hours he is missing at home with his mother. Even nursery schools sometimes take the child for long hours. 8.30 a.m. to 5.30 p.m. is not unusual. Under these conditions, where is the toddler's home life? If he goes to bed early, as he ought, his home life will be shorter than his own father's. Getting up, breakfast, tea, going to bed. When can he acquire 'good home influences' with that time-table?

We must face the fact that children who are deprived of home life and mother love at an early age are often unsettled for life. Indeed, there is a reputable body of experts on child guidance who tell us that one reason for juvenile delinquency is an early lack of parental love given in the security of the home. Delinquent children are often those who are simply revenging themselves on a world which has never given them a niche of their own.

I can hear a chorus of indignant voices: 'What rubbish! *My* child is not going to grow up a juvenile delinquent, nursery school or no nursery school.' I am sure that is true in your case, reader. But there are two points to remember. Two points we have already discussed in a slightly different form in the chapter on Punishment. Even if your child spends hours away from home at the age of two and three, and yet grows up to be a good citizen, there is still the question of whether your example may be doing harm to others less fortunate. Your child may get through the test unscathed. Others, seeing no ill effects from your case, may try the same experiments—and fail. From all points of view I think it would be a sad day for our children if nursery schools ever became the automatic destination of every toddler, the moment he had learnt to walk.

Secondly, to the confident parent to whom delinquency seems a thousand miles away, one must just say this. The parents of many 'delinquent' children were every bit as confident as you—until that horrifying moment when they found themselves in a Juvenile Court. Before that moment they had no idea there was anything seriously amiss. And yet they were confronted with the cruel fact that they had failed, somehow, at some time, in the twin parental task of *discipline* made acceptable by *love*.

It depends on the nursery school and it depends on the child. As far as the type of child is concerned, only or lonely children have obviously a special need for nursery schools and classes, provided the time spent away from home is not too long. Children who live in flats without gardens may be in the same position. The best nursery schools give valuable opportunities for companionship and free play with creative material on a large scale.

Nursery schools that function for a few hours at a time have, to my mind, an increasingly important part to play in our national life. So have all kinds of informal play-groups and play-grounds organised on a voluntary basis, often by the mothers themselves, with the help of Education Committees or other experienced people. But because the value of these things is now realised in every Mothers' Meeting, do not let us go to the other extreme and reduce our children's home life to a perilously small fragment. The mother who voted in the minority had seen a real red light, not a mere reflection of her own hopes and fears.

2 '*Freedom from their children is good for mothers.*' In certain circumstances, and in moderation, I endorse this view. It brings us back to the whole question of motherhood and career. For in some cases it may be found better for the children as well as the mother that she should try to combine the two.

Suppose a mother is completely undomesticated. Suppose she dislikes all the mundane trappings of child care. Loathes washing and ironing, cooks badly, can't dress-make, hates housework. But she's got a first-class degree in sociology! And she wants to do social work part-time. What would happen if she doggedly suppressed this side of her nature? It might actually make her a worse mother than if she went off at regular intervals to fulfil her bent.

Or to put the case on a more normal and less exalted plane—not in the world of first-class degrees but of ordinary human flesh-and-blood. (For undomesticated women are rarely as talented outside the home and as witless inside it as they sometimes imagine—or like to pretend.) Some women find the eternal round of chores, the eternal answering of children's questions, settling disputes, pushing prams, pulling on leggings and changing shoes a real strain. The children suffer, too, and get nagged instead of loved. But suppose these mothers can get some hours of release each day, or so many days a week? Then they would return to their families with zest and eagerness, their vitality and enthusiasm renewed.

A correspondent who feels this way and has literary aspirations decided recently to take a course of journalism at a London college. She finds that not only is she herself enchanted by this new interest; it has had a salutary effect on her children too! 'Apart from being a bi-weekly excursion into an entirely different world, my hobby has the effect of adding several inches to my five feet nought in the eyes of my children.'

3 '*A mother who keeps her under-fives at home will be possessive by the time she is forty.*' Possessiveness is a big subject. It may spring from many causes and develop during many different periods of life. The forties are certainly not the only danger spots.

An invalid parent may become possessive who was not possessive in good health. Again, possessiveness may be due to severe personal maladjustment, and in extreme cases may show itself in mental cruelty. Elizabeth Barrett's father—the ogre of Wimpole Street—was an example. Or again, it may be due to an emotional state which is in itself quite innocent; for instance, unwillingness to lose the company of someone dearly loved, or excessive anxiety lest the loved one come to harm while out of sight.

The Mothers' Meeting was probably thinking of this innocent kind of possessiveness when they warned the young mother about what would happen to her at forty if she hung on to her children too long ('too long' being more than three years!). The implication was that a mother who looked after her children for five whole years would never be able to acquire enough self-control to let them go when the time came for them to leave her. This is an argument carried beyond common sense. It is like suggesting that a person who regularly takes a glass of wine will become a drunkard by the time he is middle-aged; or that someone who never misses Church on Sunday is bound to die a religious maniac.

Self-control and unselfishness are without doubt necessary in order that a mother may not become possessive towards her children in later years. But a woman who has looked after small children single-handed during the first five years of their lives, is to my mind likely to develop those very qualities of self-control and unselfishness in a high degree.

The mother who was 'warned' at the meeting reacted with understandable acerbity to these strictures: her comment being, 'Are we gradually losing the sense of personal responsibility towards our children?' Another mother wrote to me on this subject with equal forthrightness from the point of view of the children: 'Why do some mothers have children, to be brought up by others in their young life? It is just the time when "Mummy" is needed. I can speak from experience, having had a very neglected childhood myself.'

To sum up the discussion of these three points, I would say this. A few hours a day organised play with other children can benefit most children round about the age of four, and also their mothers. But if a mother *wishes* to look after her under-fives herself, she is doing neither them nor herself a wrong. Quite the opposite, in fact. If a mother has enough vitality and imagination she can overcome a great many of her children's handicaps, such as having to live in a confined flat, just as well as any nursery school. A correspondent writes from Edinburgh: 'As we live in a top flat, most of my boys' games of action and adventure have to be make-believe ones. Mother usually has to join in, and each morning begins with a question. "What is it to be today? Robin Hood or Peter Pan or Dan Dare?" They never seem to get tired of them, and we all thoroughly enjoy ourselves.'

The pre-school stage lasts a very short time. It is all over in five brief years. Once school starts your child inevitably begins to grow away from you. Not only that, but he grows out of that enchanting and enchanted age when he is still 'trailing clouds of glory'. Those under-fives have an aura of innocence and sheer heaven, quickly lost, never recaptured. They are gloriously funny, gloriously natural, gloriously themselves. Nearly all children's amusing sayings, as well as many original and penetrating ones, comes before five. It seems a lot for a mother to lose, just for the sake of 'having to express herself'.

The Family Grows Up

Let us now leave the under-fives for the moment and turn to the time when the children have all grown up, or at any rate are away from home and absorbed in their own pursuits during the greater part of the day. This stage furnishes an argument for part-time careers for mothers. No woman wants to bring up a family and then be left high and dry in her early fifties with nothing to do. Nor will it be a happy situation for the children. They will have a sense of guilt at leaving their mother, who has given up everything for them, completely objectless and forlorn. If she already has a life and interests of her own it will be so much easier for them to make a graceful departure.

A woman who has been equipped for a job before marriage seems to have an obvious solution. She can 'keep her hand in' by part-time work when the children are young. Then, when the family has grown up and the house is empty, she can return to a second spell of interesting work. If, however, she has given it up completely for twenty years, she will either feel too rusty, or be too rusty, to plunge into a job again.

But the woman who accepts this reasoning—and I think the argument is a cogent one—need not think she has chosen a soft option. Two careers—family and job—are harder to run than one, whichever it is. There's bound to be a permanent state of rivalry between them. Tug-of-war for twenty years or more. You need an iron nerve, a hearty appetite, and a high I.Q., to get through.

Choosing a Career

Before deciding to embark on this strenuous enterprise of a double life, there is still one more matter to consider. *Motherhood and part-time career* sounds straightforward and definite. But it is a deceptive phrase. Not all careers will go halves with a family. Some are suitable, others not so suitable, others again very unaccommodating. It is difficult to limit and curtail one's activities in certain careers and yet still to build them up successfully against the competition of full-time workers in them, both men and women. The legal profession, already a highly competitive one even for its permanently devoted adherents, seems to be of this last type. I have never heard of a young mother managing to be a successful part-time barrister, but perhaps there are some.

Journalism, on the other hand, and writing of all kinds seem to be much more amenable. Would not girls, therefore, be wise to ponder on its possibilities before training for any particular career? The world today is bristling with careers open to women. And a very good thing that is. But if a girl of eighteen knows in her heart that she eventually intends to marry and have children, even though she has no one in particular in mind at the moment, she will do well to choose a career that is compatible with her probable future.

This means training for a profession which will (*a*) combine with marriage; (*b*) combine with a family; (*c*) be capable of suspension if necessary for a certain number of years while the children are small; (*d*) be capable of resumption at the end of that time. I suggest that among such careers are teaching, writing, art, music and entertainment; the land, horticulture and animals; and some forms of public service including politics, local and national.

It is very hard for women who have struggled for years to open the doors of all the professions to their sex, to find themselves in the end deliberately refusing to go through some of them. But that, I think, is the sensible thing to do. The frustration which such a renunciation may produce is far less devastating than a perpetual straining to 'make two ends meet' which in fact can never combine.

If, after due consideration, a young mother who has held a job before marriage, decides that even a part-time career is impossible, she may console herself with this thought—a thought that has often comforted me. Although you have abandoned an interesting job in favour of your family there is no need to harbour a secret grievance that your talents are being wasted. In managing a family a woman can cultivate every talent she has ever detected in herself—and a good many others she has never guessed at.

Are you a born story-teller? No need to look about for an outlet for your talent where there are children around. Did nature intend you for a teacher or lawyer or judge? As a mother you must combine the teaching powers of a Socrates with the subtle judgment of a Portia. This short extract from a letter I received shows how it can be done.

'When I married I became the stepmother of a little boy of four. I had in my bedroom a small statue of Christ. One day the child pointed to it and asked, "Who is that?" So I used the question as an opportunity to give the child a little religious training; ending by telling him that now he knew about Jesus he could talk to Him, especially if he needed help.

'That evening he was a very long time putting away his toys. I went along to his bedroom, to find a kneeling figure insisting that Jesus should obey him at once and put away his toys for him. I explained gently how his prayers had been answered, as I had come along to help him.'

25

The Importance of Being Father

Father and mother—he the head, and she the heart of the family. He it is who holds the ultimate responsibility for his family's welfare. He makes the final decisions. By that I do not imply that he should settle all the small day-to-day questions. Far from it. Those are best left to the mother. But he is the highest authority. And in an ancient and eternally true sense, the whole family should 'love, honour and obey' him—including his wife.

No doubt fathers had an easier time in the days of Queen Victoria, when few questioned their authority. No doubt children also had an easier time too, in one respect. For children have a natural instinct to hero-worship, and the Victorian papa was ready and willing to receive it. A woman who is now a mother herself wrote to me about her own father, who brought up eight children on 30s a week. 'The most marvellous thing to me was our exalted idea of our father. As well as loving him, we worshipped him, all through the way my mother approached him.'

But today a spirit of scepticism is abroad. Children begin to question the voice of authority at a very early age. Not only their father's authority: any voice which seems to lay down the law. Here is the authority of a father, Mr R.E. King, of Ilford, for the truth of my statement. 'My six-year-old daughter was unable to get off to sleep in a heat-wave. Having listened to the B.B.C. weather report, I went up to her bedroom just after 10 p.m. and in an effort to console, told her, quite truthfully. "The man on the wireless says it is going to be much cooler tomorrow." My daughter immediately replied, with unimaginable contempt in her voice, "Oh, they only *guess*".'

But whatever small children may appear to think of other authorities, they still instinctively want Father to be a Lord of Creation. One mother pointed out to her three-year-old daughter a fine Public Library which was being erected in her city. A team of men were putting up the big steel girders. 'Oh, that's nothing,' commented the child. 'My Daddy could easily make one of *dem*!' Kevin, at the same age, asked in a voice of keen anticipation whether his father was a tall man. When I replied that he was, Kevin remarked in a pleased and satisfied tone, 'Yes, I suppose he's as tall as a house.'

A father does not need to be strong, tall, rich or clever for his sons and daughters to admire him. You married your husband because you admired and loved him. There are things about him—a something that he *is*—which made you pick him out from all the rest of the world. It is your duty and privilege to tell his children about those things. A wife should praise her husband to her children, and *vice versa*. Parents are often far too modest these days about each other, and thus fail to give their children the indirect help and guidance they will later need in the choosing of a partner of their own. The woman who spoke with enthusiasm of her own mother's 'marvellous approach' to their father had spotted a very genuine parental function, and one that today is too frequently in abeyance.

Father Love

Little girls of three to six need to have a very close and affectionate relationship with their fathers. It is during this early period that they are unconsciously laying the basis for future happy relationships with the opposite sex, leading eventually to marriage. If, for any reason, the father fails his daughter at this stage, she may grow up with what we call an 'unresolved complex' about him. Put simply, this means that her natural early love for the first man she knows, having been thwarted, remains as a stunted growth in her heart. Festering, yet still half alive, it prevents her from ever putting forth a ripened relationship with another man.

My daughters have all, in their time, announced that they were going to 'marry Dada'. I was well satisfied that this should be so. No mother, when she hears such a remark, should tell her daughter not to be silly. She can take the opportunity, certainly of explaining that Father is already 'booked'; but she can go on to agree that he was a free man to marry, and has the virtues that some day she will look for and find in a husband of her own.

As far as young sons are concerned, Father has an equally important task. The male child needs a good 'identification' with his father. Otherwise, he will regard him as a dangerous rival in his mother's affections. Like his sister he, too, must get full and satisfying love from his parent of the opposite sex, in this case his mother, the first woman he knows. But at the same time he must learn, naturally and gently, that she is 'booked'. His father will be his pattern of manly virtues; at this stage, his hero. Later, others will come to help fill in the picture of the ideal man—older brothers, uncles, friends. But in the first few years, Father is The Man.

Discipline

It naturally falls to this Colosus to administer discipline. We have seen in earlier chapters that the whole business of family discipline and punishment is fraught with many difficulties. The child of three needs handling in a different way from the one of six. The eleven-year-old schoolboy is not the same problem, in the matter of training and guidance, as the fifteen-year-old girl. In every family both parents must learn to modify their ideas of discipline and training to suit each stage of growth, and each individual child.

Father, however, has to face yet another difficulty in the matter of discipline, which is special to him, and does not bother his wife quite so much. To put it in a nut-shell, the modern father is now always at ease in the role of disciplinarian. He has my sympathy. Why should he risk becoming the bogey man of the family by reserving himself especially for disciplinary action? Fathers are human too. They want to be loved, not feared.

In his position as breadwinner outside the home, he sees less of his children than his wife does, perhaps less than he would like. Why spoil his too-infrequent visits to the nursery or playroom with words of criticism or reprimand? Added to that, he is conscious of being a big strong man, pitted against little children. His physical power is in striking, even pathetic contrast to their childish weakness and help-lessness. If he is at all sensitive, it may well occur to him that Mother is in every way a more suitable person to administer reproof and punishment than he is himself.

Her relationship with the child is instinctively a loving and com-forting one. Even when she has to scold, her voice is soft, while his is deep and very unlike the treble tones the child is used to hearing all around him. If spanking seems to be essential, his own hand is surely too big and heavy for the job. Altogether, he feels, his reluctance to be the 'heavy father' is fully justified. Let Mother give the token tap, when necessary, and leave him free to use his size and strength as a rock for the family to lean on, a comfort and refuge in the storm.

In my view, this problem can only be solved by tact and understanding on the mother's part. And by common sense and responsibility on the father's.

'Father's wrath' is clearly an ace card up any mother's sleeve. Since Father is in fact the highest authority in the family. Mother has a perfect right to call him in as a last resort, in cases of severe disobedi-ence, bullying of other children, dangerous activities, etc. Yet she must resist the temptation to play this card too often. 'You wait till I tell your Dad . . .' Don't fling out that threat every time there is a family crisis. As one father put it, 'In my family no punishments are left over to await Father's return. If my wife could not administer justice in such an elementary way, I should get a new wife who could [*sic!*] or train the wife in the way she should go.'

Even when Father has been required to deal with a real case of insubordination, there is no need for him always to feel bound to play the 'stern parent' in the old sense. When I bring in my hus-band as a last resort I often find that his voice is quieter than mine, because he has come in from the outside and is not exacerbated by a lengthy altercation with a pack of quarrelsome children. The spark of humour, which deserts Mother all too early in the fray, is Father's most effective weapon. As a relative outsider, he may spot that the bully is in need of a little consolation and encouragement himself, rather than a thunderbolt of punishment delivered by the family Jove from the heights of Mount Olympus. The appeal judge is not infrequently kinder and more merciful than the lower court. Father's role, if he combines common sense with responsibility and loyalty to his wife, may often turn out to be a gentler and more congenial one than is generally supposed.

However, even in these days of lax parental discipline, I still come across fathers who err in the opposite direction. They are too stern. Nervous or fearful children can be greatly supported by a calm, sympathetic father; but their already anxious disposition will be further disturbed by a father who sternly tries to suppress their fears. Indeed, many children who say they are afraid of the dark, of burglars, bogeys or ghosts, are in reality afraid of an unduly harsh or repressive parent. The parent whom they long to love, but whose strict attitude keeps them at arms' length and fills them with secret alarm, is externalised in the form of some terror of the imagination, like the enchanted prince in the fairy-tale who was turned into the shape of a bear.

When the nervous child happens to be a boy, the father is under an even stronger temptation to deal with the case by 'firmness' than when it is a girl. He feels that he himself is being shamed by such an unmanly son. A tendency on his wife's part to 'give in to the child' must, he thinks, be counteracted by extra firmness on his own. In the old days this attitude was prevalent among fathers. A correspondent from Shropshire recalls her childhood terrors, and how her father mistakenly tried to make her 'face up to them'. 'I was one of ten children; large house; dark cupboards; antique lighting; older children frightening younger ones. Father made me go on errands to bedrooms in the dark to conquer my fears. I suffered greatly in consequence.'

Today many fathers still feel their wives are 'spoiling' their children if they sit by them until they fall asleep. A case of this kind was

quoted in the chapter on Night Fears. But the mother who instinctively feels it is cruel to leave a child to cry alone, is in the right.
Father can play a real and valuable part in helping their children to
'face up to' life. But they will not succeed if they adopt the 'sink or
swim' method of throwing them, alone and helpless, into the very
situations which they dread.

Setting an Example

Some fathers, with the best will in the world, find that they just
cannot make their discipline effective. A father who had been faced
with serious trouble in his family wrote with genuine bewilderment:
'Where did I go wrong? On reviewing myself, I find I have used
strong-arm methods, gentle persuasion, kindly talking, in fact every
known method of bringing up a large family.'

Every known method? One other method still remains. It was
familiar to our less humble, perhaps less sensitive ancestors. But
the modest father of today too often forgets it. It is the method of
example.

To try to be an example to his sons is not conceit on a father's
part. It is his duty. I suppose the disagreeable mental picture we have
of the typical Victorian papa partly accounts for the modern father's
self-effacement. Remember that portly, unctuous, complacent *pater
familias*? Not a congenial father-figure today. Yet personal example is
still Father's strongest weapon. Far stronger than a 'strong arm'.

The Victorian father's instinct to set a good example to his children and be a pattern for his whole family to copy, was a correct
one. The trouble was that the example he set sometimes turned out
to be bad rather than good. Instead of being a model of gentleness,
tolerance, courtesy, altruism, sincerity and modesty, he ended by
presenting his family with a living portrait of harsh, dogmatic, selfish hypocrisy. Not that all our great-grandfathers and grandfathers
were like this. But some undoubtedly were. And literature seized on
these types, embellished them lavishly, and handed them on to their
descendants as objects of scorn and fear. The pendulum has swung

far against Father as Head of the Family. Now he feels it is perhaps safer not to try to set an example at all, rather than risk the odium of setting a bad one.

It is true that a father's deliberate efforts to set himself up as a lighthouse before his children seem to involve some danger of damaging his own character in the process. One instinctively feels one's little light is safer under a bushel, than held up aloft with a gesture at once priggish and puny. But because a father is conscious of his own imperfections, that is no reason why he should throw in the sponge altogether, climb down from his pedestal and metaphorically grovel about on the floor on all fours with the immaturest members of his family. It is one thing to admit to your children that you sometimes make mistakes. It is quite another to abdicate from leadership entirely, for fear of falling into sins of pride and pomposity.

This business of the patriarchal pedestal is an important one. The real question for Father is not whether to get on to a pedestal or not. His children will put him there anyway, at least during the first few years of their lives. The important point is how he spends his time up there. And whether he is able to descend gradually, at the right moment; and at the same time give his sons and daughters the necessary leg-up into their own niches of manhood and womanhood.

In most families both parents have to face the pedestal problem to a greater or lesser extent, though the father's special position of authority combined with relative remoteness, makes his problem particularly acute.

'Mummy, I shall never forget the first time I thought you and Dada weren't perfect,' said Judith a short while ago. 'It was awful. Like not believing in Father Christmas any more.' She is not worried about our perfections or imperfections any longer. For now she is mature enough for us to discuss them openly together. But there was a time, not so long past, when she confesses to having gone through horrible doubts about us.

Some parents seek to get out of the difficulty by saying, 'Don't get on to a pedestal at all. Then your children will be saved this experience.' They make special efforts to keep on their children's level. They even decide that the children shall call them by their Christian names instead of 'Father' and, 'Mother'. A friend of mine writes to assure me that much as he might like to climb on a pedestal for the strange and edifying experience, he would feel it quite impossible to do so. 'My children would laugh their heads off if they thought I was up to anything of that sort.'

I think these parents are mistaken. The modest father quoted above I happen to know is on a very high pedestal indeed. To his children he is a 'city set on a hill'. The very fact that he frequently says 'Sorry' to them when he makes a mistake, laughs at himself, and takes their advice as well as giving his, keeps him there.

Those who consistently refuse to give their children the happy experience of looking up to something on an eminence are doing neither themselves nor their young ones a service. Even, it may be, the parents who protest their intense discomfort at the very idea of a pedestal are in truth suffering from a distinct touch of characteristic pride. They will not climb up lest their feet of clay should get exposed and chipped in the course of a hurried and forced descent.

The correct and natural descent may take place at different ages according to the individual child. I told my seven-year-old daughter the other day that I had made a mistake. 'Mothers and Fathers often make mistakes,' I added purposefully. She goggled a bit over this. But chiefly over my admitting it. She had evidently noticed the fact already herself. Then I went on to say that parents sometimes did wrong things, and had to be sorry for them, as she did when she was naughty.

This was a big shock. She drew in her breath, and I could see a new relationship was dawning. But the distinct glint of pleasure in her eyes told me that I had taken the first step down from the pedestal none too soon.

Of course it is important not to descend prematurely either. The toddler puts his parents on a pedestal for a sound reason: he *needs* them there. It is essential for his security to feel them beside him and yet above him—the absolute perfection of love and wisdom.

As we have already seen, there is only one sensible way of spending those precious short years while you are up aloft. In setting a good example. But you are no more than human if you find it a considerable strain always trying to behave well in front of the children.

It is Saturday afternoon. Father is playing tennis with his young ones. He slips and comes a cropper. A stream of language slips out too. 'And Daddy won't even let me say "blast!"' is his son's private comment. Most children understand extreme provocation, and there are two perfectly sound ways of dealing with this situation. If you think swearing is permissible for adults but unseemly in children, you say, 'But Daddy's a *man*! It's all right for him.' Swearing then becomes a grown-up privilege to look forward to, like smoking, staying up late or driving a car. But if you think swearing is bad in itself, there is only one thing for it. Daddy must apologise.

I have found from experience there are two kinds of bad example which specially shake our children's faith. One is a sudden outburst of temper or uncontrollable rage. Children like us to be absolutely reliable and utterly calm. They are struggling so hard for stability themselves. How devastating if parents are violent and temperamental too!

Antonia, at twenty-one, can still remember with horror a friend's mother suddenly boiling over, rushing at her daughter and shaking her furiously for some minor offence. She felt this display was 'letting down the parents' side'.

Unfair punishment is the second kind of bad example which children cannot tolerate. They have a mania for 'fairness'. They expect to be punished sometimes, but it must be fair. Occasionally my husband and I let our children suggest their own punishments. This shows them that we are ready to go out of our way to find a punishment which they themselves think adequate and fair. It also reveals to the parents, often in a striking manner, how differently from us they rate their misdemeanours. Kevin, at the age of five, suggested 'No more pocket-money for a year', as a punishment for taking and losing his sister's pencil. But Patrick, at seven, proposed being fined the meagre sum of 3d for smashing up a fine stone garden pedestal with a coal hammer. Perhaps the pedestal was symbolic of parental power and he felt we should really be paying him, rather than fining him, for letting off his resentment in no worse way! We must now leave the pedestal, and return to consideration of Father's specific role.

Father as Judge

How far should fathers be expected to solve family problems, settle disputes, give judgement in quarrels? One of Father's problems is that he is bound to be in some degree an Absentee Head. Away at work, he rarely sees the start of a family rumpus. He has to pick up details, as best he can, from biased witnesses. So do not always expect the wisdom of Solomon.

One thing he particularly dislikes. To be greeted with a tale of woe the minute he gets home. 'Bob won't do his homework today. . . . Do make Susan promise not to stay out late again. . . . The light's fused in the bathroom. . . . David won't have his lunch at school. He says they poison him, and he wants to take sandwiches every day. But they say they can't make exceptions . . . ' This certainly unburdens Mother. But it is not the way to greet a weary, homecoming breadwinner. It is better for the tactful wife to bottle up her grievances at least till after tea. By then Father should be braced to take it.

If you force him to scold the erring members of his family before he has had time to hug them, what will be the result? Ten to one he will give them a very perfunctory scolding, and you will feel let down. But the opposite tactics are just as fatal. The tactics which consist in insulating the tired father as completely as possible from the rush and tumble of family life. Some wives, particularly those who have a slightly overmaternal feeling towards their husbands, actually encourage their man to isolate himself behind a newspaper the whole evening. Too much slipper, pipe, and fire-side cosseting, puts that 'paper curtain' between him and the rest of the family.

Father should not be treated as a neurotic invalid, to be protected from the facts of family life. Often, he is only too eager to wash his hands of the whole thing. As one mother wrote, troubled by difficulties with teenage children, 'My husband does not do a thing about it; in fact he won't talk to me about it at all.' A sensitive wife should realise there are some moments when it is tactful to dwell on the children's successes, the funny or charming things they have said or done that day, rather than the number of times they have quarrelled with each other and disobeyed her. At other times it is quite safe, and in fact the very best possible tactics, to draw Father right into the heart of the family whirlpool. He has a part to play at every age, and on every subject—with the babies as well as the teenagers; on sex and religion, homework and finance.

Family Finances

Finance is a subject of general family concern which wives find it hardest of all to raise. At least, to raise tactfully, at a psychological moment. I sometimes feel there's never a *good* moment for discussing that budget problem. The only difference is that some moments are worse than others. Personally, I find the middle of the week-end the least inappropriate. If you wait till then you are not rushing it. And there will still be plenty of time to get over it so that the week-end finishes on a cheerful note.

Some misguided fathers are secretive about their income. They regard it as 'my own affair' instead of a family affair. Of course they thus avoid all unpleasant talk about money with their wives. But theirs is not a 'marriage of true minds'.

It would not be right or necessary to tell children all about their parents' financial position. They must not be made to worry about shortages which are not their responsibility, or alternatively, to get a kick out of affluence which is in no way due to their own merits or exertions. But there is no doubt that children do take a distinct interest in all problems of £. s. d., and family finance. It is right that they should do so. The earlier they learn about the world's work, the better. I always tell my children the price of things I buy for them, when they ask me: even sometimes the cost of presents (though it is better not to teach them to judge a gift by its money-value).

If Father is the approachable type, his children will be only too glad to discuss with him the intricacies of finance, and at all stages to assist him with suggestions for the spending of the family income. Alwyn, aged four, had just been told Mummy had gone to hospital to bring back a new baby for the family. Alwyn pondered on the new responsibilities involved, and asked: 'How much did you win on the football coupons, Daddy?' 'About twelve pounds,' his father replied. 'Oh, I thought it was thousands,' said Alwyn. 'You will have to pull your socks up.'

A father from Carshalton reports the following ingenious suggestions from his six-year-old son:

'Daddy, why don't you buy a car?'

'Because I'm buying a house, so I can't afford a car as well.'

'But if we sell our house, how many cars could we buy with the money?'

'Three or four.'

'That would be one car for Mummy, one for you and one for me.'

'But then where would we live?'

'Well, you could sell the fourth car and buy another house.'

26

Father and the Family

'My husband is just not interested in children—at least, not till they reach their teens.' How many of us have heard some such expression of opinion from our friends? Or even, on occasion, found ourselves tempted to use it? A wife sometimes makes a virtue out of necessity. Because her husband appears at first to show little taste for baby-worshipping, she allows him henceforth never to get involved in nursery problems, persuading herself that a 'real man' is naturally uninterested in nappies, spinach puree and the best type of drop-side cot.

This is a fallacy. The father who seriously desires his family to grow up a success must take a hand in the children's upbringing at every stage. A sensible mother will draw him in from the very beginning, refusing to be put off by his initial diffidence or reluctance to explore again the long-forgotten country of childhood. Men have their pride. Often they keep out of the nursery for fear of seeming ignorant or clumsy. A modicum of tact and encouragement on the wife's part should end these difficulties. If only fathers would realise that to be 'just not interested' is a dereliction of duty, what a much more balanced and happy affair family life would be!

Let us try to follow this 'problem parent', sympathetically through the four stages of his fatherhood.

1 He's Allergic to New-Born Babies

Nature is partly to blame. She has allowed Father (unlike Mother) to maintain a certain detachment. If the new-born face is red and creased, it will not look pink and smooth to him. Its voice at 2 a.m. will not be a tug at the heart-strings. It will sound exactly what it is: a piercing and implacable impediment to sleep.

Of course some mothers profess to feel every bit as objective and detached towards the new baby as their husbands. But I believe most of them do not really mean what they say. They are adopting an inno-cent device for concealing their unbounded and illogical pride in an offspring whose appearance is clearly very rudimentary. When my first baby arrived, with a touch of jaundice and a magnificent bone-structure of face and head, I referred to her apologetically in front of visitors as 'Gandhi'. But privately, in my own mind, I could already see close resemblances to Helen of Troy and Queen Guinevere.

The slight feeling of detachment which is natural to a father before birth and in the early stages may have been increased by other factors. A happy and devoted husband, he may have seen no need to increase the family circle even by one child, and thus risk spoiling the close relationship between himself and his wife. On a lower level, he may just have felt a selfish fear of getting less comfort and atten-tion than he did before.

Charles Lamb, the essayist, wrote a moving story of his 'dream children'; the unborn, phantom family whom he longed for and saw, as ghosts, clinging round his arm-chair in the evenings. But the father who knows a baby is more likely to be a reality than a ghost, may feel exactly the opposite to Charles Lamb. He may see his corner by the fire becoming a less cosy place. There will be no time to put out his slippers. A fire-guard hung with airing clothes will keep off the pleasant warmth from his knees. Altogether, he's allergic to babies.

A husband who discourages his wife from having children is taking on a grave responsibility. Nothing else can make up to a woman for the child she wants but is not allowed to have. I have known a case where the husband, who did not want children, noticed with satis-faction that his wife was exceptionally house-proud. He concluded quite erroneously that she did not wish for a baby around, 'messing up the place'. In another case, the husband noticed his wife was moping, and rightly concluded she wanted a baby. However, he felt that her maternal instincts could be satisfied by something else not quite so drastic. So he presented her with what seemed to him a perfectly adequate substitute—a charming Persian cat!

In the first case, the husband stuck out, and there was always an air of indefinable but genuine sadness in that home. In the second, he regretfully decided the cat was not enough and became the father of four children.

Fathers who at the outset have rejected the idea of babies are often excessively attentive, anxious about their welfare, even possessive, when they come. They think every slight cold is going to turn into pneumonia; every set-back at school indicates a complete failure. The children are not allowed out in wet weather for fear of getting a chill, or in hot, for fear of sun-stroke. A bicycle is denied them lest they should get run over; and at a later stage, lipstick is forbidden the girls for fear of attracting undesirable boy-friends.

All this excessive worry must be due to the father's early rejection of his offspring. For the rest of their childhood he feels secretly guilty at not having really wanted them. He tries to ease his own conscience by treating them with exaggerated attention and solicitude. A father who finds himself worrying unduly over his children and unable to give his growing sons and daughters their natural freedom, should think back to the beginnings of his fatherhood. Then he will be able to stop over-compensating for dislike or indifference, and become the good parent he wants to be.

It is not true, of course, that every man who is against having children and later worries and fusses over them when they arrive, is suffering from a hidden sense of guilt. Some men, like some women, are born worriers. They cannot face the responsibility of children. They worry at the thought of a child before it arrives, and continue to worry over its welfare afterwards. Fortunately, the man with an over-anxious temperament is often aware of this weakness before he becomes a father, or even a husband. He naturally gravitates towards a woman with a complementary and well-balanced temperament.

Before the children arrive she will instinctively help him to smooth out his anxieties about himself. After they arrive it will be her job to allay his anxieties about them too. In many cases this type of man is gifted with sympathy and sensitivity. Given the right help, and a happy family life, he generally turns out in the end an excellent father.

Once the new baby has arrived, the wife can greatly help her husband to develop the right attitude towards it. Or rather, she can do much to prevent extraneous factors from increasing his original indifference or even aversion to the baby.

During the first month a husband is often ousted, quite unintentionally but unmistakably, by his own child. Up to the baby's arrival he and his wife are extremely close together. She is dependent on him as never before. Suddenly all this is altered. A new world—an entirely female world at that—collides with his self-contained planet. He begins to suspect his wife now depends on her own mother more than she does on him. Certainly she has put herself unreservedly into the hands of the nurse. The baby—*his* baby—undoubtedly, to him, belongs to this monstrous regiment of women. It is his worst month. He is suffering the tortures of the 'unwanted father', the 'deprived parent'.

None of this need happen. But it is up to his wife to prevent it. A mother who has had several children gradually discovers this for herself. She learns to make a special point of including her husband in the magic circle round her bed. If he wants to return to sleeping in the same room with her, or in the same bed if they have been used to this, there is no reason why he should not do so, a day or two after his child's birth. The more he feels he is 'in at the beginning', the better it will be for the young family.

His wife must handle her beloved court firmly. There must be no atmosphere of 'women's business', secret conclaves or sudden hustling of Father from the room because Mother is tired or baby is going to be fed, or he is in some other way *de trop*. If his wife is careful to avoid any such occurrences, there will be no injury to parental feelings through being 'dropped at birth'. We all know the tale of the child who is backward through being 'dropped at birth'. Many a father is 'backward' in his parental duties and pleasures for the same reason.

Most mothers, with their first babies, are blissfully unaware that this sort of thing is going on. It was not until the birth of our third child that I realised how far from ideal had been my husband's first few weeks with the two elder ones. He had indeed seen his first child born, and stayed for the second till the doctor turned him out. But on the third happy occasion, when the doctor accidentally arrived late, the proud father was able to enter into the spirit of the drama by opening the sealed maternity drum—no mean achievement for agitated hands!—and generally assisting his second son into the world. In the weeks that followed, and later when other babies were born, he was not 'turned out', either physically or in a deeper sense.

Of course, mother and child are bound to be the centre of attention during the first days and weeks. Every woman feels this is her finest hour. She deserves to make the most of it. But she must recognise that her own exaltation should not mean her husband's isolation. She can be the centre, without driving him to the circumference and beyond.

If she fails to draw him in, she cannot expect a perfect father in the days to come. He will tend to connect babies in his mind with weeks of boredom and exclusion. And she will soon be saying, 'My husband is just not interested . . .'

After the first month is safely over, fatherhood begins in earnest. Happily, the old idea that a man cannot be trusted to hold a baby because he might drop it, is dying fast. The jeweller who fixes the inside of a lady's wrist-watch, the gardener who sets a delicate seedling, the veterinary surgeon who examines a kitten or puppy or lamb, is surely able to handle a human baby. I have often noticed at christenings how naturally and competently the priest holds his small bundle, while it is the young godmother who is afraid she is going to drop it.

The humble father is sometimes surprised at his own *expertise* when an emergency forces him to take over the baby for a time. A distinguished professional man was landed with his four-month-old son when his wife went down with 'flu during the week-end. 'I found I could do everything, including bathing, except make a "lap",' he said afterwards, 'and that was the fault of my trousers! So I dried him and changed him on the bed.' The experiment was indeed such a success and so popular with the baby, that his wife, in the next room, began to notice the absence of crying during bath and dressing time. She called out to know if anything was wrong!

On Father's side, he need not fear that the time he spends with a very young baby is wasted—that it is so 'inhuman' before the age of six months or so as to be unable to distinguish between parents and strangers, or to know whether the man who is holding him is his father, or the postman.

Contrary to the belief of many young people, a three-month-old baby is able to tell the difference between friend and stranger. On one occasion, when Catherine was just that age, an acquaintance paid us a visit, and seeing the baby, remarked philosophically; 'Isn't it strange to think that this child in two years' time will be a human being with powers of intellect far outstripping any animal, however old and intelligent? Yet now it is less intelligent than your dog. Why, unlike the dog, it can't even tell "it's master's voice" or face!' I promptly handed the baby to this stranger to hold. In a moment her face crinkled and she began to cry. My friend was astonished. We tried the experiment several times, including in our trial a woman who was a children's nurse, but whom the baby did not know. Each time she cried in the arms of a stranger, but stopped when her mother took her again.

Of course not all children are as sensitive as this. Babies of three or four months old are usually quite happy to be held by anybody or everybody, as long as they are not squeezed too tightly or held so loosely that they feel they are going to fall. It is generally not till nine months or more that they show strong aversion to being held by strangers. By the fact that they do not mind being picked up by a stranger at three months, does not mean they do not *know* he is one.

Children's intelligence, like all their other powers, develops imperceptibly. We usually make the mistake of underrating rather than overrating their progress. Of assuming they have not reached a stage of consciousness which in fact they have. To my mind the dog analogy is a misleading one, in any case. At no stage in their development are babies 'just like animals'. So Father, if he wisely decides to spend time with his young baby, can rest assured that he is from the start in the company of a real human being.

2 Fathers Prefer Toddlers

Many a father who thinks he cannot abide babies changes his mind when they grow into toddlers. 'I like them when they get interesting,' he says. Which really means, when they can walk and talk. This interesting age also happens to be the most mischievous one. By mischief I do not mean naughtiness, which implies the deliberate intention to do what is clearly understood to be wrong. Children *are* capable of being naughty—contrary to the view of some psychologists—but not at the toddler stage. Mischief, however, is the toddler's occupational disease. I define mischief as: Enterprise which takes the wrong turning.

Fathers are particularly suited to tolerating this 'enterprise' without mistaking it for naughtiness. Of course it is easier for them to be broad-minded. Mothers usually have to clear up the mess. But here is the story of a father who encouraged initiative in his toddler—and bore the consequences nobly! It is sent by his wife. 'Dad always laughed at his three-year-old son's antics with the car. When Mother complained of screws being out he would say, "He is a budding mechanic." One day, in a hurry to get to the factory, he found the petrol tank had been filled with water from the duck-pond. Dad reluctantly paid the bill, but still laughs about it.'

As we saw in the last chapter, the girl of about three begins to enter into a strong emotional relationship with her father. She goes through a stage of being 'married' to him, and often expresses her feelings for him, either explicitly or symbolically, to her parents. A three-year-old from Swindon created a 'Daddy' for her teddy-bear. 'Teddy's Daddy,' writes her mother, 'goes to work with my husband in the back of the car. He goes night-flying when my husband does, and returns to sleep the following morning, when he must on no account be disturbed. Now, it appears, he has gone to Australia in an aeroplane—as has my husband—and together my daughter and I lament their combined absence.'

A father who takes the trouble to cultivate his toddler will get not only her love, but also the benefit of those many wise-cracks and funny remarks which are too often heard by mothers only. Here is a five-year-old from Wellingborough watching her father putting up a flypaper in the kitchen. 'What are you doing, Daddy?' 'Putting up sticky paper to catch the flies.' 'You should put that up in the dark, Dad. The flies can see you put it up in the daylight.'

A small girl from Hythe, Kent, wanted to learn how to knit. To encourage her, her mother gave her a ball of white wool and started her off with a few rows. She persevered in silence for some time, but it was not till her father came home and asked what she was doing, that she made one of those revealing remarks which show us the child's world in all its magical illogicality. 'I'm knitting a vest for my baby sister, and I hope it turns out to be a *pink* one!'

This reminds me of one bath-time when Antonia was three. Her father came in, and in the course of conversation I said to him, 'I hope her eyes are not going to change from blue to grey'—my own sad fate! 'I'm afraid they are, Dada,' said Antonia, 'I'm afraid they are going to change to pink.'

One cannot overstress the good which fathers can do by taking an interest in their very young daughters and sons. In many cases they do not realise the depth of the children's feelings towards them. Perhaps the following stories, all drawn from perfectly normal families, will help to illustrate the point.

Small children are acutely aware that their fathers are away from home more than their mothers—more than they would wish. They worry about what is happening to Daddy when he is not safely under their eye. In their imagination they see him injured, or otherwise in danger. Most of us mothers must have noticed how often, in childish games of 'Mothers and Fathers', the father has an accident; how seldom the mother.

A Manchester girl of four likes to pretend she is the mother of a family. 'I have to ask her,' writes her own mother, 'how the different members of the family are keeping. When it comes to the husband, he's always had a bad finger. But after being pricked with a needle by the doctor, he is back at work. On being asked what kind of a job he has got, it is always, "Oh, a very good job. He's selling papers on the station."' Here are anxiety combined with love and pride in a typical mixture.

Another four-year-old from East London noticed that his father had been playing football rather more often than usual. Very small children who watch their fathers playing rough ball games are apt to be extremely agitated by the apparent danger they run. When Antonia, at the age of just two, first saw her father in a rugger scrum, she shouted to him in great trepidation, 'Out, Dada! Come out! Out!' She could not say many words, but these were enough to express her feelings. The child in the following story, being older, was able to give vent to his fears in a fantasy based on, and no doubt exaggerated by, a chance phrase he had heard. Here is the story as told by his mother:

'After Daddy had played three games of football in one week, our eldest child came into the kitchen, wearing a scarf and an old handbag slung satchel-wise round his body. "Hello, Lady!" he said to me, "I'm on my way to school." (He had not started school yet.) "I will have to stay at school all the time," he added wistfully. "Really?" "Yes, my Daddy has died. He died playing football. He died with his boots on ..."'

Children whose fathers have to be away from home often miss them more than we imagine; far more than they themselves are able to express to us in words. A father who has been absent for some time may well be taken in by the apparently casual way in which his offspring greets him on his return. Because a child goes on playing with his bricks when his father comes into the room, and has to be told by his mother, 'Look, here's Daddy! Come and give him a nice hug'—this child may in fact have missed his father sorely. Children's behaviour does not always follow the adult pattern. The child who just raises his head from his building blocks enough to say, 'Daddy, help me balance this one on top of the roof,' may be as pleased to see his father as the child who has learnt, either from copying older children, or from instruction, to rush up at once from whatever he is doing and fling his arms round his father's neck.

We must learn to decipher our children's inmost feelings from signs and hints rather than form formal protestations of affection.

Such outward displays are delightful when they do come. But Father must not be disappointed if his child gives little or no direct indication that she has missed him. In all probability she has. Here is a four-year-old from Worthing, Sussex. Her father was away at the war and she missed him deeply. But how did she express her feelings? By telling her mother that she was not her real mother. 'I've got a "France" mother, and she's called Mrs Leave. I live with Mr and Mrs Leave.' Note the significance of the word *leave*. Her father had left her, so she sorrowed. But when he came back to see her, he was 'on leave'. No wonder she summed it all up, and comforted herself, by living with Mr Leave.

There is no need to emphasise the ways in which a father who is naturally 'good' with little children can add to the fun and happiness of his family. Given imagination and the will to help, there is no father so unskilful and 'bad with his hands' that he cannot make an important contribution to the magic world of early childhood. The child's own imagination will supply what is technically deficient. A lady who is now a mother herself remembers the happiest moment of her early childhood being largely due to a father who set his imagination to work in unison with his child's. 'At the age of three my maternal instincts came to the fore. Having found the old leg of a table in the shed, I brought it indoors, tenderly wrapped in a shawl, and insisted that it was a baby. I took it to bed with me. Imagine my surprise when I awoke to find my baby had acquired beautiful blue eyes, rosy cheeks and a rose-bud mouth. My father had most obligingly painted on a face while I slept.'

3 Father the Family Film Star

When a boy reaches school age he will be looking around for a hero. Perhaps he will choose a character from television. More than likely it will be his own father. This is the stage when a boy's admiration for his father attains its peak. At eight or nine he still thinks his father is perfect. It is not until he reaches double figures that he finds out the sad truth. That Father is not better at everything than anyone else!

Thus, his father is now in the most commanding position he will ever achieve for influencing his son. Discipline can still be enforced, though time is running short. All the problems we discussed earlier under Obedience and Punishment are his to solve. 'Do's and Don'ts' are still in place; but if this opportunity for character training—for teaching in no uncertain manner the difference between right and wrong—is let slip, it will never come so naturally or so easily again. So fathers, do not fail your children now, through not being 'interested'.

On one point, however, the father of schoolchildren needs some sympathetic understanding. In all probability this is the stage when his family is costing him most. He feels the burden of being the breadwinner most acutely. He spends longer at work turning that extra penny. He comes home more tired in the evening.

Without doubt a man's home is the proper place for rest and recreation. During the week-ends and holidays he rightly expects to enjoy himself, to recoup his energies for the next round. How is he to square his legitimate desire with his duty to spend time with his older children?

For we must remember that the schoolchild is not always quite so superficially engaging as he was a few years ago. Gone is that winning frankness; he is less spontaneous and amusing, not quite so attractive to look at or so confidingly companionable.

It is all very fine to invite a man, however weary, to walk round the garden holding the hand of a charming three-year-old who really wants to be told the names of flowers and where Daddy intends to plant his next row of peas. Even if the enthusiastic toddler imitates his father a little too faithfully, his parents are ready to treat it with the indulgent laugh. 'My son of nearly three,' writes a mother who became a victim of father-imitation, 'was watching me strain peas, beans and new potatoes for dinner. The front door bell rang and when I returned to the kitchen all the peas and beans had vanished. My son led me into the garden, scratched at the earth and said, "I've planted them, Mummy, like Daddy did." When my husband came home we all had a good laugh.'

But when it comes to dealing with the tousled ten-year-old, after the usual skirmishes over hands, face, neck and ears, Father may well feel he has done his duty for the day, and put his feet up. Even the imaginative games of older children may prove irksome. As one mother put it: 'My husband enjoys some of it, but gets annoyed if they go on too long.'

Here is one answer to the problem. It has been said that 'the family which plays together stays together'. Play is only one strand among the many which bind together family life. (Families which can pray together as well as play together are in a strong position.) But play is undoubtedly one which will help Father in this particular dilemma. Let him take some trouble to do things with his sons and daughters, to play games with them *which he himself enjoys.* This is not selfish; it is sensible. Children between childhood and the teens are avid for every kind of experience. It will be surprising if they do not follow Father in at least some of his favourite recreations, provided he gives them a lead.

If he likes golf, let them begin to learn. If it's walking, mountaineering, fishing, let them be initiated early into the joys which he can share with them. If he dislikes sight-seeing but still finds it fun to kick a football around, let him concentrate on the thing that gives him recreation and pleasure. A sensible, practical father will make it easy for himself to enjoy the company of his children. If he takes the trouble to think these things out while the children are still small, and plans a little ahead, he should have no insuperable difficulty in doing the work of a true father in his home and at the same time finding there the necessary recreation from the day's work outside it.

4 Father Tackles the Teenager

Fathers who wait to be interested in their children till they reach their teens are playing a dangerous game. A boy of fifteen is not going to be easily swayed by a comparative stranger. Particularly if that stranger has been living in the house all the time. How can fathers expect suddenly to become intimate and influential? All the same it is better, as I have said before, to jump in at the eleventh hour than not at all. For the teens are an awkward age for the mother to cope with single-handed. With boys it is the age when they normally break free from their mother's influence. It is a critical time. If their father fails them, who knows what substitute will step in?

Girls are often hysterically emotional at this stage. The strength and calm affection of a man—their father—is what they need.

In earlier chapters we discussed some of the special problems confronting youth. Problems of independence, discipline, pleasure, depression, and many more. Others there are which find no place in this brief collection—problems of training, for instance, in religion and sex, both subjects of the deepest importance. How to teach these; whether a parent should teach them himself, or whether they are better left to somebody else; whether sex can be tackled on its own or should be related to religion—all these questions open up wide new areas for discussion and decision. In all of them the father's role is a vital one.

No limit exists to the stream of problems which pours over him as his children pass from school to work. Sometimes, like the procession of kings in *Macbeth*, their endlessness appals. At other times their sheer insistence spurs him to feats of ingenuity and perseverance that would have seemed impossible in his carefree bachelor days. Necessity may be the mother of invention. Family life is certainly the father of resourcefulness.

Fatherhood Today

It would be wrong to end without a word of warning. Even more may be required of Father in the future than was wanted in the past. He must face the fact of the Emancipation of Women. The feminist revolution has had its representations on family life. In the old days when women were tied exclusively to the home, there was at most one absentee parent—Father. Mother was always there, devoting the whole of her superabundant energies to the problem of her domestic kingdom. Today this single-minded or confined life (whichever way you look at it) is over for most women, either in wish or in fact. Nor do I believe the clock can be put back. For reasons already set out in Chapters 23 and 24, I am myself in favour of mothers having some life outside the home.

But this raises a difficulty. If mother and father are both to be absentees, the family is in danger of neglect. There are people, welfare workers and others, who point even now to the harmful by-products of this increasing social tendency.

Father has it in his power to provide part of the solution. If women are to enjoy more freedom men must take more responsibility. Father must come more fully into the family, now that his wife has established her right to moments of existence outside it.

At this point a second warning is due—to wives. By 'father coming fully into family life', I do not simply mean that he should help with the washing-up or do more chores. A man will only be interested if he has real responsibility and power of making decisions. Men slipped into the habit of 'leaving everything to the wife' because, while they themselves were working, the women were on the spot and knew all the facts. If men are now to come right in they must have a real say in all that goes on. The privilege of wielding a dish-cloth is not enough.

Let us get rid of kitchen-slaves and *haus-fraus* by all means. But the omnipotent matriarch must go too. Let both types make way for the balanced mother and father of the future. In their spiritually equal partnership lies the true hope of the family.

Under the terms of this partnership there will still be divisions of labour. The man will earn most of the bread, his wife will still do most of the cradle-rocking. Mother will be more in evidence during the earlier years, when the giving and receiving of love is first priority. Father will step up his influence at the toddling stage, developing the process of discipline, made acceptable by love. By the time the child is seven or eight he should know how to love and how to obey; but long before this he will already have started on his third stage, learning the difference between right and wrong.

Slowly, as the years pass, he discards the natural selfishness of infancy. Gradually he emerges with altruistic feelings and a social conscience. At three he automatically searched for and took the biggest cake on the plate. At ten he had learnt to leave the very biggest for somebody else. It still seemed illogical to do so (*'somebody's got to have the biggest; why not me?'*) but he knew by now it was 'the done thing'. At nineteen he is voluntarily collecting funds for famine-struck people he has never seen.

All through this long process *both* his parents have been offering him help in the three chief ways at their disposal—love, discipline and example. (They may indeed be conscious of a fourth kind of help, and set it above the rest. Remembering their many failures and shortcomings in the upbringing of their family: reading, as we all do, the sad stories of juvenile delinquency and crime—they may well be moved to say with humility and fervour, 'There, but for the Grace of God, go I ...')

Bookish talk about education and upbringing often gives a false impression. It seems to suggest that the various duties of parents should be performed in watertight compartments; or at separate stages in the child's life; or tidily split up between father and mother. When love ends, discipline begins—or so it appears. When father steps forward, mother steps back. Mother gives and receives love. Father gives discipline and receives obedience.

Of course every practising parent knows this schematic blue-print of upbringing is nonsense. The emphasis may indeed vary from stage, from parent to parent, from child to child. But the child needs two parents always, throughout his life. And all the factors of upbringing are present, either in embryo, in course of development, or predominantly, all the time.

Most particularly must the love of both parents be there from the beginning. Love must never fly out of the window; certainly not when discipline comes in at the door. In building up the family, love comes first, last and always. It is at once the foundation-stone, the mortar between bricks, the pinnacle crowning the whole.

When difficulties arise in the teens and we grope around for cords to hold the family together, there is only one cord stronger than the pulls of novelty and excitement. That cord is love.

Childhood is past. Adolescence is nearly over. Anxious parents are wondering whether old ties will hold against the strain of new influences, or whether the moment the years strike twenty-one, youth will be off. Let us give freedom with both hands, secure in the knowledge that youth is still, in the words of Christina Rossetti, 'a captive in thy cord. Let that cord be love'.